BASS AND UPRIGHT BASS MASTERY

A Complete Guide to Timing, Technique, and Dexterity

Bass Guitar, Upright Bass, and Contrabass

MUSIC MASTERY SERIES, VOLUME 5

By Tad Sisler

This book is dedicated to the extraordinarily talented musicians I've worked with over the years. Your insight and intelligence pushed me to become more rounded and precise. Thank you all from the bottom of my heart for making me a better player and person.

TABLE OF CONTENTS: PAGE

FOREWORD

I grew up in a musical environment. My mother, **Elaine Witt Sisler,** was a child prodigy pianist. At the age of 17, she was already a soloist for the renowned *Chicago Symphony.* As early as I can remember, she taught me music theory and how to play the piano. Before I was a teenager, I was earning superior ratings in classical piano competitions.

Tad Sisler's Mother Elaine Witt Sisler at Age 16
Source – Sisler Private Collection

When I was 12, I was placed into the choir at my school because the band already had a piano player. I discovered I could sing, and quickly, I earned a scholarship to *ISOMATA,* an excellent music school in Idyllwild, CA, which, at the time, was affiliated with the *University of Southern California.*

After moving to live with my father in Missouri, I was selected to *the Missouri All-State Choir* in my senior year of high school. I pursued a music career, and I've been performing, producing, composing, and recording for almost fifty years.

In my twenties, I had the honor of working with **Frank Sinatra**. I studied music and choreography under **Jacque D'Amboise.** I've opened for my band in huge stadiums for artists, including **Kenny Rogers**, and I've worked with the titans of the music industry onstage and in recording studios. As an author, I recently won a coveted **Reader's Favorite Award** for a biography I wrote on the life of a famous trumpeter.

I've recorded bass players of all types on tracks in many different genres. I developed a solid left hand to play keyboard bass on my gigs, and I became very proficient at it, although there will never be a substitute for a real bass player.

Learning to play bass is more than just technique and theory. It's learning to know the instrument so well that you can play in the pocket and drive an entire band or orchestra; the feeling you get from doing that is unmatched.

The best things in life don't come easy, especially at first. You will excel beyond your wildest dreams if you desire to do this. This book will serve as your guide, drawing upon the advice and wisdom of the masters who came before you, leading you toward knowing your instrument and being able to perform in any situation. We will delve into different genres, including rock, jazz, and classical, to give you a complete picture of the instrument and to help you understand all facets of bass playing in your unique journey to play what you want at the highest level. Stay with it and enjoy the process. I promise it will be worth it!

Medical Disclaimer:

The information provided in this book is intended for informational and educational purposes only and should not be used as a substitute for professional medical advice, diagnosis, or treatment. Always seek the advice of your physician or a qualified healthcare provider with any questions you may have regarding a medical condition or before beginning any new health, fitness, exercise, breathing, or dietary regimen.

The exercises, techniques, and suggestions in this book may not be suitable for everyone and could result in injury or adverse effects. If you have an existing health condition or suspect you may have one, consult a licensed medical professional before attempting any of the practices outlined herein.

The author and publisher explicitly disclaim any responsibility for any adverse effects, injuries, or damages that may result from the use or misuse of the information presented in this book.

Legal Disclaimer:

The author and publisher have made every effort to ensure the accuracy and reliability of the information contained in this book at the time of publication. However, errors, omissions, or inaccuracies may occur. The author and publisher make no guarantees regarding the completeness, reliability, or applicability of the information provided. They explicitly disclaim any liability for any loss, damage, or disruption caused by errors, omissions, or actions taken based on the content of this book, regardless of the cause, including negligence or accident.

The content in this book is provided for general informational purposes only and does not constitute professional advice of any kind, including medical, legal, or financial advice. If you require specific guidance, please consult a qualified professional in the relevant field.

The author and publisher make no guarantees or promises regarding the effectiveness, results, or outcomes of any techniques, strategies, or recommendations presented in this book. Readers are responsible for using their own judgment and discretion when applying the material in their personal or professional lives.

Further, any external quotes, references, online courses, books, or products mentioned in this book are for informational purposes only and do not imply endorsement, approval, or promotion by the author or publisher. The inclusion of such material does not constitute a guarantee of quality or effectiveness.

INTRODUCTION

My father once told me that most people are either good at many things or excellent at one thing. He urged me to choose one thing and to become the very best at it. It always astounds me when I encounter individuals who excel at multiple things, especially in today's multitasking world. In my career, I've had the privilege of meeting and collaborating with bass players who are equally proficient on bass guitar as they are on upright bass, but this is a rare occurrence. Most bassists typically excel at one or the other. However, there are exceptions, and **Victor Wooten** is a shining example of this. He has mastered all versions of the bass.

ARTIST SPOTLIGHT
VICTOR WOOTEN

Victor Wooten is a prime example of an iconic bass player. He excels on bass guitar, fretless bass, and upright bass. As a teenager, **Wooten** not only mastered the four-string bass but also five- and six-string basses. He also worked on expanding his harmonic range and exploring more intricate chord voicings and soloing techniques. As a result of his hard work and practice, **Victor Wooten** became a sought-after session musician in Nashville.

In his early twenties, **Wooten** joined **Béla Fleck and the Flecktones**, a band that blended bluegrass, jazz, and funk. The band's fusion of genres encouraged **Wooten** to experiment even more, and he began to work on mastering the fretless bass. The fretless bass, with its smooth, sliding tones, gave **Wooten** a new way to express himself melodically, and he incorporated it into his playing to bring out more nuanced, vocal-like lines.

As his career evolved, **Wooten** also began to explore the upright bass. Despite having mastered the electric bass, the upright bass presented new challenges. Unlike the electric bass, the upright is a purely acoustic instrument, demanding different finger techniques, stamina, and an entirely new approach to tone and intonation. As most great musicians do, **Wooten** took to it with the same curiosity and passion as a child. Moving over to upright bass also brought him closer to the roots of jazz, and he began incorporating the instrument into his performances, especially during acoustic or jazz sets.

Today, **Victor Wooten** is not only a virtuoso on the bass but also a teacher and philosopher of music.

He founded the *Victor Wooten Center for Music and Nature*, teaching students how to play bass and connect with music on a deeper, spiritual level. His book, *The Music Lesson,* is a must-read.

In the book, **Victor** emphasizes that mastering an instrument is about more than technique—it's about emotion, creativity, and connection. **Victor Wooten** became a master of all types of bass through dedication, curiosity, experimentation, and passion.

Victor Wooten
Credit: Ryan Bodenstein | Flickr | Creativecommons.org

MASTERING PERFORMANCE SKILLS

Confucius said, *"Choose a job you love, and you will never have to work a day in your life."* The journey of mastering an instrument, filled with hard work and dedication, can also be the most exhilarating part. As you work to master technique, timing, and performance skills, you will encounter obstacles and frustrations, but these are part of the learning experience. If you follow a step-by-step structure, regardless of your current skill level, you will improve and eventually master your instrument, experiencing the joy of musical mastery.

Learning to play the bass is not all technique: mindfulness in practice will accelerate your growth as a musician; learning to handle stage fright and becoming a better player will naturally foster confidence within you.

In this book, I will guide you to master techniques for multiple instruments, teaching you to confidently switch between bass guitar, upright bass, and contrabass, should you choose to play all. Many bassists aim for versatility, allowing them to perform across genres and in many different musical contexts. This ambition for versatility will open new musical horizons for you, even if you choose to focus on just one of these instruments. The most important thing you can learn to be a sought-after musician is impeccable timing and rhythm skills. Practice will help you ensure your basslines are tight and rhythmically precise. Bass is a core component of any rhythm section. This book will focus on developing your ability to play perfectly in time through practice with metronomes, click tracks, and mindfulness techniques.

I will also help you to build the confidence to perform live. Performance anxiety can be easily remedied with a few techniques and mastery of your instrument.

Performing live is a huge aspect of musicianship, and playing confidently is invaluable.

SELF-DISCIPLINE

Many people have told me, *"I always wanted to learn how to play bass, but I have no self-discipline."* Self-discipline is not something you have or don't have. It's something you make happen. Whether you're a religious person or not, you can understand the concept that when God created us, we were given this amazing power to choose, a power so strong that we actually can use it to choose against God if we want to. I understand the power of addictions, but we can choose to overcome smoking or drugs, or anything we put our minds to. Self-discipline is your choice. You can become the best at what you do if you decide that there is no other option but success. This all starts with self-discipline, with your choice to make it happen, and then to persist until you've succeeded. It's that simple. If you don't believe you can learn an instrument, you probably won't. But I promise you, if you follow the wisdom and resources of this book, you will find your way if you stick with it.

I will bring in the wisdom of the great performers to help you accelerate your growth and become an outstanding performer and recording artist. I hope you will find as much pleasure and solace in your music as in my illustrious career. No matter where you are in terms of skill, you can benefit significantly from this book. This book unfolds from the ground up, so if you're already proficient, you'll find some of the early chapters to be elementary, but I promise you will still find gems of knowledge that will help you as an overall player. Let's move forward together into this amazing world of music performance! As you study the music and techniques that were created before you picked up the instrument, look forward to carving out a new consciousness about the instrument and its nuances. As my dear friend, multi-platinum songwriter and performer **Sergio Mendes** said:

"I hope those great melodies become popular [again]; that the new kids hear the old melodies and enjoy them."

Sergio Mendes and Tad Sisler
Source – Sisler Private Collection

You are the bridge to our future.

CHAPTER ONE
THE BASS INSTRUMENT

T he bass may be the most important instrument of a band or orchestra. Bass anchors the foundational rhythm and harmonic structure, and anchoring the music with its deep, resonant tones that bridge rhythm and melody.

A study published in *Frontiers in Psychology* found that musicians who master multiple instruments, including different bass types (electric bass, upright bass, etc.), demonstrate significantly enhanced cognitive flexibility, problem-solving skills, and musical adaptability compared to those who specialize in just one instrument, allowing them to seamlessly switch between genres and performance styles.

My sister, **Suzanne Ramsey**, was a trained psychologist and a mental health center director for many years. She told me that she found in many patients that simple stress and burnout were the cause of many mental health issues. Fears, including fear of failure or disappointment, were other leading issues beyond simple depression based upon loss. Learning to sing or play an instrument can help to alleviate many mental health issues, and a recent study in *Science Daily* showed that playing an instrument and learning music have been linked to better brain health in older adults. My sister had many tools to help her patients, and music therapy was among those tools.

Suzanne Ramsey and Tad Sisler
Source- Sisler Private Collection

After a very close family member of mine contracted Parkinson's disease, I did an enormous amount of research to help her, and in the hopes that I would not eventually also get the disease. I researched vitamins and supplements, but the most revealing thing I found was that playing an instrument and constantly pushing your brain to learn the nuances of the instrument can be a deterrent to Parkinson's and dementia.

A 2024 British study conducted as part of the **PROTECT** dementia research project, which involved over 25,000 older adults, revealed that playing an instrument helps improve memory and executive function. These activities help build cognitive reserves, potentially delaying or preventing age-related neurological conditions.

Additionally, the study highlighted the benefits of music therapy and instrumental training, showing that they can enhance brain plasticity. This ability to rewire neural pathways plays a vital role in maintaining cognitive health and combating the progression of neurodegenerative diseases like Parkinson's.

The increasing recognition of the role of musical activities in public health strategies for aging populations is a testament to the proactive approach to boosting brain health and delaying cognitive decline. This realization makes music not just a form of entertainment, but a powerful tool for neurological wellness, inspiring us to take charge of our cognitive health. So, in effect, there's a chance you may be saving your own life by becoming proficient at an instrument!

My father, **Maynard Lee Sisler**, was a physician specializing in internal medicine. He learned medicine on the spot as a medic on a Navy ship in World War II. Doctors were scarce in the South Pacific, so my father quickly learned to diagnose sailors and do emergency surgery when needed. Years later, after extensive training in medical school, he told me that the most important thing a doctor can do is to listen to their patients. In their own way, they will tell you what you need to know to help them. I believe it's the same with all of us. We must learn to listen to ourselves and what our body and mind tell us. Most of what is wrong with us can be helped immensely by exercise, eating right, and getting enough sleep.

Maynard Lee Sisler, M.D., F.A.C.P
Source – Sisler Private collection

"When you go on a stage — or even in a café or a room — and you play it's all happening right then and there: the exchange, the art, the communication. Performance is in the moment." — Gail Ann Dorsey

Gail Ann Dorsey
Credit — Rosana Prada/Flickr/creativecommons.org

HISTORY OF THE BASS

The bass instrument has a long history that spans centuries, evolving from its early origins into the modern upright bass, contrabass, and bass guitar used in today's music.

ORIGINS AND EARLY DEVELOPMENT

The bass most likely originated in the Renaissance and Baroque periods (16th-17th centuries), where early versions of stringed bass instruments emerged. These early instruments, like the **viola da gamba** (a fretted, bowed instrument), provided low-pitched harmonic support in ensembles. The **violone**, an ancestor of the double bass, was larger and deeper in tone than other instruments in the viol family and began to be used for basso continuo parts in Baroque music.

DEVELOPMENT OF THE MODERN UPRIGHT

By the 18th century, the double bass, as we know it, had started to take shape. It was influenced by the violin family (with a curved shape) and the older viol instruments (which sometimes had frets)—the instrument's tuning was standardized to E-A-D-G, similar to the bass guitar. The upright bass became a staple in orchestral music, providing the low-end foundation for classical compositions. Its size, typically ranging from 3/4 to 4/4 size, made it suitable for a wide range of musical genres.

CONTRABASS

Contrabass is often used interchangeably with "upright bass" or "double bass." Still, technically, it refers to instruments tuned an octave lower than a standard bass or with an extended range. In orchestras, contrabass parts often add extra depth to the bass section. The **contrabassoon** and **contrabass clarinet** are examples of other contrabass instruments, but the term usually refers to the largest bowed bass instruments for string players.

BIRTH OF THE ELECTRIC BASS GUITAR

In the 1930s, the **electric bass guitar** was invented but wasn't popularized until the 1950s when **Leo Fender** created the **Fender Precision Bass**. This invention provided a more portable and louder option for bassists, making it easier to be heard in modern amplified music. The bass guitar uses the same tuning as the upright bass (E-A-D-G) but is played horizontally, typically with fingers or a pick. The electric bass soon became essential in genres like rock, jazz, funk, and pop.

MODERN VARIATIONS

Today, the **upright bass** plays a prominent role in classical, jazz, and some folk genres, while the **electric bass guitar** dominates rock, pop, and other modern music styles. Additionally, various specialized basses, such as **five-string basses** (adding a lower B string) and **fretless basses**, can mimic the sound of an upright bass.

SECTION ONE: TYPES OF BASSES AND EQUIPMENT REQUIREMENTS

BASS GUITAR

The bass guitar is a stringed instrument, generally guitar-shaped, primarily used in genres like rock, jazz, reggae, funk, and pop music. It typically has four strings, but five- and six-string versions are common.

A bass guitar's body is solid or semi-hollow, and electric models typically use wood like alder, ash, or maple.

The bass guitar has a long **neck** with frets like a guitar (except for the fretless bass), allowing players to fret notes precisely. The **headstock is** the top part of the guitar that holds the tuning pegs for tightening and loosening the strings.

Pickups are electronic components on electric basses that capture the strings' vibrations and send them to an amplifier. The **bridge** is where the strings anchor onto the body of a bass guitar. **Strings** for a bass guitar are typically steel or nickel. They are much thicker than guitar strings, producing rich, low frequencies, and four-string basses are tuned to E-A-D-G.

UPRIGHT BASS (DOUBLE BASS)

The upright bass is the largest and lowest-pitched acoustic string instrument, primarily used in classical, jazz, and folk music. A smaller, electric version of the upright bass, made by *Ampeg*, was used heavily in recording and stage performing since the 1950s. New electric upright basses are exciting and featured in the next section. The **body of** the acoustic upright bass is hollow, large, and resonating, made of carved or laminated wood (or a hybrid between the two). The **neck** is long, without frets, requiring more precision and ear training to play in tune. The **fingerboard** is curved and unfretted where the player's fingers press the strings.

The **bridge** is tall, lifting the strings above the body. The **tailpiece anchors** the strings on the body of the bass. The **endpin** is an adjustable metal rod at the bottom, supporting the instrument when standing or seated. The **strings** are typically thicker and longer than those of bass guitars, made from gut, synthetic materials, or steel. Most upright bass strings are tuned to E-A-D-G, the same as a bass guitar, but they have a much longer vibrating length.

CONTRABASS

The contrabass refers to a few different instruments, but in the context of this book, it's the contrabass guitar, a sub-range of the double bass family. The contrabass is usually tuned an octave lower than a standard bass guitar. It might have a similar shape to the bass guitar but is usually much larger. The neck and strings are longer and heavier to handle the lower frequencies. The contrabass is typically used in experimental or niche music styles, sometimes in classical music, and is rarer than traditional basses.

DIFFERENCES BETWEEN INSTRUMENTS

The upright bass is much larger than a bass guitar, and the contrabass is larger still in most cases. The bass guitar is played in a horizontal position while sitting or standing with a strap, and the upright bass is played either standing or seated.

Bass guitars are usually fretted, while upright bass and contrabass are fretless and require more precision. Bass guitars are common in modern rock, pop, and funk music, while upright basses dominate classical, jazz, and folk genres. Upright basses come in different sizes. Most adults and growing youth play a ¾ size bass, or full-size bass. ½- or 5/8- size basses are available for people with height under 5 feet 4 inches. 4/4 size basses are available but huge.

UNIQUE BASSES

Basses also come in unusual styles. The most prominent is the **Chapman Stick**, a unique stringed instrument invented by **Emmett Chapman** in the early 1970s. It is designed for **two-handed tapping**, where both hands tap the strings on the fretboard to create notes and chords, rather than the traditional method of plucking or strumming. This allows the musician to simultaneously play **melody, harmony, and bass lines**, making it a versatile instrument for solo performances or ensembles.

The Chapman Stick typically has **8 to 12 strings**, half of which are tuned for bass notes and the other half for melody or chords. Its extended range and tuning suit various musical genres, including **jazz, progressive rock, classical, and experimental music**.

Musicians like **Tony Levin** (known for his work with **King Crimson** and **Peter Gabriel**) have popularized the instrument, showcasing its ability to blend seamlessly into **rock and ambient music**. The Chapman Stick is prized for its ability to add a **unique textural element** to music, enabling performers to create complex arrangements that would be difficult to achieve with traditional instruments.

Chapman Stick
Credit – Picasa 2.6/Wikimedia Commons

BEST ELECTRIC BASS GUITARS

By best, I mean the most popular used by pros for different genres:

Fender Precision Bass: A rock, jazz, and pop music standard.

Fender Jazz Bass: Known for its versatility and rich tones, it is a favorite among jazz and funk players.

Music Man StingRay: Popular in rock and funk for its punchy tone.

Ibanez SR Series: Lightweight with fast necks, popular among modern players.

Yamaha TRBX174: Excellent 4-string electric bass guitar. **Yamaha** has other excellent models too. More great brands include **Shecter** and **Glarry**.

BEST UPRIGHT BASSES (ACOUSTIC)

Kay Bass: Known for its vintage sound, often seen in bluegrass and jazz.

Thompson Upright Basses: Quality instruments handcrafted for classical and jazz musicians.

NS Design Electric Upright Basses: Modern design for electric amplification with the feel of an acoustic upright bass.

Other great upright basses are **Ibanez Bass Workshop, Yamaha RBX 375,** and **Peavey Millenium BXP**.

CHOOSE THE RIGHT PICKUPS

Choosing the right pickups to enhance your sound is equally as important as choosing the right bass. Pickups are generally interchangeable, and most of my friends modify their basses with better pickups than the factory models. By best, I mean the most popular for different basses:

SINGLE-COIL PICKUPS are known for their bright and articulate tone. They produce a crisp, clear sound with a defined attack, making them suitable for jazz, funk, and classic rock genres.

BEST SINGLE-COIL PICKUPS

Fender Custom Shop '60s Jazz Bass Pickups: These are highly regarded for their vintage-style tone, capturing the classic sound of 1960s Jazz Bass models.

Seymour Duncan Quarter Pound P-Bass Pickup: Though designed for a Precision Bass, it offers a high-output single-coil option that adds punch and clarity to the sound.

SPLIT-COIL PICKUPS, often found on **Precision Basses**, consist of two single-coil halves wired in reverse polarity to cancel out hum. They produce a thick, punchy tone with a solid low-end and midrange presence.

BEST SPLIT-COIL PICKUPS

Seymour Duncan SPB-3 Quarter Pound P-Bass Pickup: Known for its high output and enhanced bass response, this pickup is a favorite for rock and punk players who want a more aggressive tone.

Fender Original P-Bass Pickup: This model captures the vintage warmth and roundness of early Precision Basses, suitable for genres like blues, classic rock, and Motown.

HUMBUCKER PICKUPS use two coils wired in opposite directions to eliminate noise and hum. They produce a thicker, fuller sound with more output than single coils, making them ideal for heavier styles such as metal and hard rock.

BEST HUMBUCKER PICKUPS

EMG 35DC: An active humbucker known for its powerful output and clear, extended frequency response, popular among metal bassists.

Nordstrand Big Split: This pickup offers a hybrid design that combines elements of single-coil and humbucking tones, making it versatile and suitable for various genres.

SOAPBAR PICKUPS can house single-coil or humbucker designs and are named for their rectangular, "soapbar-like" shape. They provide many tonal options, from warm and rounded to punchy and bright.

BEST SOAPBAR PICKUPS

Bartolini MK-I: Often found on mid-range basses, these pickups are known for their smooth and balanced tone across the frequency spectrum, making them suitable for jazz, fusion, and rock.

Aguilar DCB: These passive soap bars offer a dynamic, full-bodied sound with plenty of clarity and definition, perfect for players seeking versatility.

ACTIVE PICKUPS incorporate a built-in preamp and require a battery. They offer a higher output, greater tonal shaping options, and typically lower noise levels. They are commonly used in modern rock, metal, and funk.

BEST ACTIVE PICKUPS

EMG P/J Set: This active pickup combination includes a Precision-style split-coil for the neck and a Jazz-style single-coil for the bridge, offering versatility and powerful output.

Seymour Duncan Active EQ Bass Pickup Set: Known for providing a wide tonal range, including punchy lows and crisp highs, suitable for a variety of genres.

FACTORS TO CONSIDER IN BASS PICKUPS

Genre: The style of music you play can significantly influence the type of pickup you need. For example, jazz and funk players may prefer the clarity of single-coils, while metal players might opt for high-output humbuckers.

Tone Preferences: Decide whether you want a vintage, warm sound or a more modern, high-output tone. This will help you decide whether you should use passive or active pickups.

Bass Guitar Type: Your specific bass model will often dictate the types of pickups that can be used (e.g., P-Bass split-coils or Jazz Bass single-coils).

Choosing the right equipment is important, but I've seen great bassists make even mediocre equipment sound great with the right amount of adjusting, tuning, and master playing. Music is a significant part of who we are.

Kim Deal is a great rock and indie bassist, playing with **The Pixies** and fronting **The Breeders.** Kim summed it up in this statement:

"To my mind, there is a reason that music is there, and it's about being human."

Kim Deal
Credit- Wikimedia Commons

BEST UPRIGHT BASSES (ELECTRIC)

NS Design - WAV, CR, and NXT Series: Known for their playability, portability, and modern design, at different price points. Patented Polar™ pickup system allows for bowing and pizzicato styles to be clearly distinguished.
Yamaha – SLB300 and SLB200 Series: Highly respected for replicating the feel and sound of an acoustic upright bass. These models feature high-quality electronics that produce rich, realistic tones suitable for practice and performance. The SLB300 has a resonance chamber to more accurately simulate the acoustics of a traditional upright bass.
Other great brands are **Eminence, Kala,** and **Alter Ego.**
Stagg EDB Series: Affordable option for starters on electric upright bass. Popular for their simplicity, decent sound quality, and easy portability. Lightweight and highly portable.

FOR TRADITIONAL UPRIGHT BASS PLAYERS SEEKING AN ELECTRIC OPTION:

KNA Pickups: KNA pickup systems allow musicians to electrify an acoustic bass without sacrificing tone, serving as a hybrid solution.
Fishman is one of the most well-known brands for acoustic instrument pickups, including upright bass pickups. Their **Full Circle** pickup is highly regarded for its natural, transparent sound and adjustable tone, making it suitable for jazz, classical, and other styles.

The **Realist** pickups, designed by bassist **David Gage** and **Ned Steinberger**, are favored for their ease of installation and natural sound reproduction. The **Realist Copperhead** is one of the most popular models, known for its warm tone and balanced output.

K&K Sound specializes in piezo pickups for acoustic instruments. Their **Bass Max** model is a popular choice among upright bassists for its simple installation and clear, punchy sound, suitable for various genres from jazz to rockabilly.

BEST CONTRABASSES

Ibanez BTB Bass: Offers extended range and lower tuning, popular among experimental bassists.

Warwick Rockbass Alien: An acoustic-electric hybrid bass that can handle a wide frequency range.

STRINGING YOUR BASS GUITAR

Start by threading the string through the bridge, then wind it around the tuning pegs, ensuring it's tight but not overly stretched. You'll need a new set of bass strings, appropriate for your instrument's scale length; wire cutters or pliers for trimming excess string; a tuner.

CLEANING YOUR BASS

Regular cleaning prevents dirt, sweat, and oils from accumulating on your bass, which can affect both its appearance and functionality. After each playing session:

Wipe Down the Body and Neck: Use a soft, dry cloth to remove fingerprints and smudges.

Clean the Fretboard: Occasionally clean the fretboard with appropriate cleaners and a clean cloth, especially when changing strings.

Polish the Hardware: Gently clean metal parts to prevent corrosion.

REMOVE OLD STRINGS

Loosen the strings by turning the tuning pegs until the tension is released. Unwind the strings entirely, pulling them out from the bridge and tuning pegs. Safely discard the old strings. This is a good time to clean and condition the fretboard while the strings are off.

INSTALL NEW STRINGS

Start with the thickest string (the low E) and proceed to the thinnest (G). Insert the String into the Bridge. For most basses, you'll thread the string through the back of the bridge or body (depending on the design). The ball end of the string should securely rest in the bridge or tailpiece.

Pull the String to the Tuning Peg by pulling the string along the neck and inserting the free end into the appropriate tuning peg's hole.

Leave some slack for winding, about 2-3 inches, to allow the string to wrap around the tuning post. Wrap the String Around the Tuning Peg: Begin winding the string around the tuning post, ensuring that the string wraps downward as you turn the peg. This creates tension and helps the string stay securely in place. Make sure the string winds neatly and doesn't overlap itself on the tuning post. Using a tuner, bring the string up to pitch. The standard tuning for a 4-string bass is E, A, D, G (low to high). Continue the process for each of the remaining strings, moving from the thickest to the thinnest. After all the strings are installed and tuned, gently stretch each string by pulling it away from the fretboard and then retune. This helps stabilize the tuning. Use wire cutters to trim the excess string from the tuning posts, leaving a small length to avoid sharp ends.

CHANGING STRINGS AND SETUP ADJUSTMENTS
STRING CHANGING:
Frequency: Change strings every few months or sooner if you play frequently. Old strings can sound dull and are more prone to breakage.

Types of Strings:
- **Roundwound**: Bright tone, suitable for most genres.
- **Flatwound**: Mellow tone, preferred in jazz and Motown styles.

Installation: When changing strings, ensure they're wound correctly to maintain tuning stability.

SETUP ADJUSTMENTS:
Truss Rod Adjustment: Controls the neck's curvature. A properly adjusted truss rod ensures comfortable action and prevents fret buzz.

Action (String Height): Adjust the bridge saddles to set the string height for ease of playing.

Intonation: Adjust the string length at the bridge so each note plays in tune up the fretboard.

Professional Maintenance: Consider periodic setups by an experienced technician to keep your bass in top condition.

UNDERSTANDING AMPLIFIERS AND EFFECTS
BASS AMPLIFIERS are designed to handle low frequencies. They come in combo amps (amp and speaker together) or separate head and cabinet setups.

Controls:
- **Gain/Input Volume**: Sets the level of the input signal.
- **Master Volume**: Controls the overall output level.
- **Equalization (EQ)**: Shapes your tone by adjusting frequency bands.

EQ Settings:
- **Bass (Low Frequencies)**:
  - **Boost**: Adds depth and fullness.

- **Cut**: Reduces boominess in certain rooms.
- **Midrange**:
  - **Boost**: Enhances presence and punch.
  - **Cut**: Creates a scooped sound typical in slap bass.
- **Treble (High Frequencies)**:
  - **Boost**: Adds clarity and definition.
  - **Cut**: Softens harshness.

COMMON EFFECTS PEDALS

Compression:
Function: Evens out volume levels and adds sustain.
Use: Essential for maintaining consistent dynamics.
Overdrive/Distortion:
Function: Adds grit and harmonic richness.
Use: Popular in rock and metal genres.
Chorus:
Function: Creates a shimmering, multi-layered sound.
Use: Adds depth, commonly used in funk and pop.
Envelope Filter (Auto-Wah):
Function: Produces a vowel-like, dynamic effect.
Use: Signature sound in funk and jam band music.
Octave Pedal:
Function: Adds a note one octave below or above.
Use: Thickens the sound, useful in solos or to mimic synth bass.

TONE PRODUCTION
TECHNIQUES TO ACHIEVE DIFFERENT TONES

Adapt to playing different genres with different tones.

PLAYING TECHNIQUES

Fingerstyle:
Tone: Warm and natural.
Use: Versatile, suitable for jazz, blues, rock, and more.
Variations: Altering plucking strength and position affects tone.

Slap and Pop:
Tone: Bright, percussive.
Use: Essential in funk, R&B, and some pop music.
Technique: Thumb the string (slap) and snap it with a finger (pop).

Pick Playing:
Tone: Sharp attack, bright.
Use: Common in punk, metal, and some rock genres.
Variations: Different pick materials and thicknesses affect tone.

HAND POSITIONING
The placement of your hands also can help to modify tonality.
Near the Neck:
Tone: Fuller, bassier sound.
Use: When a warm tone is desired.

Near the Bridge:
Tone: Tighter, more defined.
Use: For a punchy, articulate sound.

INSTRUMENT SETTINGS
Determine your sound by choosing the right pickups and adjusting your tone.
Pickup Selection:
Neck Pickup: Warmer tones.
Bridge Pickup: Brighter, more focused tones.
Blend: Combining pickups offers tonal versatility.

Tone Controls:
Passive Basses: Tone knob cuts high frequencies.
Active Basses: May have onboard EQ for boosting/cutting frequencies.

STRING CHOICE
The material and gauge of your strings will also affect your tonality.
Material:
Nickel-Plated Steel: Balanced tone.
Stainless Steel: Bright and crisp.

Gauge:
Lighter Strings: Easier to play, brighter tone.
Heavier Strings: More tension, fuller tone.

GENRE-SPECIFIC TECHNIQUES
For every new genre, you will want to adapt your sound. Here are some time-honored techniques for three popular genres:
Jazz:
Technique: Smooth fingerstyle, use of flatwound strings.
Tone Shaping: Emphasize midrange for warmth.

Rock/Metal:
Technique: Aggressive pick playing, potential use of distortion.
Tone Shaping: Boost lows and highs for a powerful sound.

Funk:
Technique: Slap and pop, percussive elements.
Tone Shaping: Crisp highs and scooped mids for clarity.

ARTIST SPOTLIGHT
PAUL McCARTNEY

Paul McCartney
Credit – Jerzy Bednarski, creativecommons.org

Paul McCartney was an innovator who changed the trajectory of pop and rock music. He was born on June 18, 1942, in Liverpool, England. **Paul's** band **The Beatles** redefined rock and pop music in the 1960s. In partnership with **John Lennon**, he co-wrote some of the most cherished songs in history. A unique aspect of his musical journey is his left-handed bass playing, a rarity in rock music. Being naturally left-handed, **McCartney** initially grappled with playing the guitar until he discovered he could flip a right-handed guitar upside down and re-string it to suit his dominant hand.

McCartney's left-handed bass playing was not just a quirk but a defining element of **The Beatles'** sound. In the early days, he wielded a **Höfner 500/I** bass guitar, a choice made for its symmetry and comfort for a left-handed player. His melodic bass lines and his unique playing style were instrumental in shaping **The Beatles'** musical trajectory. Songs like *"Something"* and *"Come Together"* from **Abbey Road** are testament to his innovative approach to the instrument. **The Beatles** looked more symmetrical on stage because **Paul's** bass jutted out in a different direction than the right-handed guitars of **John Lennon** and **George Harrison**. Unlike many bassists of his time, **McCartney's** playing was rhythmic, melodic, and dynamic, often serving as a secondary lead instrument in many of the band's songs.

Following **The Beatles'** breakup in 1970, **McCartney** started his successful solo career. He formed the band **Wings** with his wife, **Linda McCartney**, and continued to produce hit songs and albums throughout the 1970s. Although most people identify **Paul** with his vocal and songwriting prowess, **McCartney's** left-handed bass playing remained a cornerstone of his music. Even in his solo career, his continued use of the **Höfner** bass became one of the most iconic images in rock history.

Paul McCartney went on to play many instruments. He is one of the greatest and most prolific songwriters of all time. **Paul** pioneered the left-handed bass and changed the direction of pop music with his lyrics and melodies, along with the brilliance of his producer, **George Martin.**

STRINGING A LEFT-HANDED BASS

While the basic steps for stringing a right—or left-handed bass are the same, the key difference lies in the direction of tuning and string wrapping.

Right-Handed Bass: When tuning a right-handed bass, turn the tuning pegs counterclockwise to tighten the strings (raise the pitch). The string wraps clockwise around the tuning peg (viewed from the top of the headstock).

Left-Handed Bass: To tighten the strings on a left-handed bass, you turn the tuning pegs clockwise. This reversal is due to how the headstock and tuners are oriented on left-handed instruments. The string wraps counterclockwise around the tuning peg. This action ensures the tension is applied correctly when tuning, preventing the string from slipping.

The bridge on a left-handed bass is often mirrored to accommodate the opposite direction of string tension. This does not affect the stringing process, but you will need to ensure that the strings are correctly threaded through the bridge or tailpiece. Exercise caution when purchasing a used bass on eBay or other sites. Many poor quality or damaged basses are sold at discount prices, and they can be disappointing when you try to play them.

BEST STRINGS FOR YOUR INSTRUMENT
BASS GUITAR STRINGS

Ernie Ball Regular Slinky: A popular choice for rock and metal.
D'Addario NYXL Bass: Known for durability and consistent tone.
La Bella Deep Talkin' Bass Flats: Flatwound strings, preferred for smooth jazz tones.

UPRIGHT BASS STRINGS

Remember when stringing to feed the string through the tailpiece and secure it at the pegbox. Upright bass strings need to be stretched over the bridge carefully to avoid damage.

Thomastik-Infeld Spirocore: A hybrid string that works well for both pizzicato (plucking) and arco (bowing).
Pirastro Evah Pirazzi: Popular for classical players for their rich, warm sound.
D'Addario Helicore: A versatile option suitable for jazz and orchestral playing.

CONTRABASS STRINGS

Stringing is similar to the upright bass, but make sure the strings are well-suited for the extended range.

D'Addario XL Chromes Flatwound: Perfect for maintaining tension and clarity in low tunings.

DR Strings Fat-Beams: Known for a deep, rich tone, preferred by funk and jazz bassists.

KNOWING YOUR INSTRUMENT

BASS GUITAR

Bass guitarists use many techniques depending upon the style of music, each contributing to the versatility of the instrument:

Fingerstyle: The most common method, where players pluck the strings with their index and middle fingers, allowing for precise control over dynamics and tone.

Slap and Pop: Popular in funk music, this technique involves slapping the strings with the thumb and "popping" them with the index or middle finger, producing a percussive and punchy sound.

Picking: This method, often seen in rock and punk music, involves using a plectrum (pick) to play the strings. It offers a sharper, more aggressive tone.

Tapping and Harmonics: Tapping and harmonics are advanced techniques that significantly enhance a bassist's expressive range. **Tapping** involves using one or both hands, tapping the strings against the fretboard, which produces notes without plucking or picking. This technique allows for rapid note sequences, extended arpeggios, and complex melodies by treating the fretboard like a keyboard, enabling the execution of passages that are challenging with traditional fingerstyle or pick methods. **Harmonics** are ethereal, bell-like tones produced by lightly touching the string at specific nodal points (such as above the 5th, 7th, or 12th frets) without pressing it down entirely, then plucking or tapping it to excite the harmonic overtones.

There are two types: **natural harmonics**, played on open strings at these nodal points, and **artificial (or false) harmonics**, which involve fretting a note and simultaneously touching a nodal point relative to that fret.

Combining tapping with harmonics enables bassists to create shimmering textures, intricate melodic lines, and ambient soundscapes, pushing the instrument's capabilities beyond conventional bass roles and adding a unique sonic dimension to their playing. **Palm Muting** involves resting using your palm, or the side of your picking hand, on the strings near the bridge while you're playing, creating a muted, rhythmic sound. It is frequently used in genres like reggae and rock.

BASS GUITAR - ROLE IN DIFFERENT GENRES

Rock: The bass guitar often follows the chord progression, locking in with the drums to create a driving rhythm. Iconic bassists like **Paul McCartney (The Beatles)** and **John Entwistle (The Who)** demonstrate how the bass can act as a melodic instrument, adding depth to rock compositions.

Funk: The bass takes a lead role in funk music, with slap and pop techniques creating a rhythmic and percussive groove. Funk bass lines are characterized by syncopation and complex rhythms, exemplified by artists like **Bootsy Collins (Parliament-Funkadelic)** and **Larry Graham (Sly and the Family Stone).**

Country: In country music, the bass guitar provides a steady and simple foundation, often playing the root and fifth notes to support the chord changes. This creates a solid, rhythmic "walking" feel, familiar in classic and modern country tracks.

Jazz: The bass is central to jazz, including fretless bass guitar. It often plays walking bass lines that move through scales and chord tones, offering both rhythmic and harmonic support.

Jazz bassists like **Charles Mingus** and **Jaco Pastorius** demonstrate the instrument's ability to improvise and take on melodic roles.

"Making the simple complicated is commonplace; making the complicated simple, awesomely simple, that's creativity."
– Charles Mingus

Charles Mingus
Credit – Flickr/Creativecommons.org

Latin: In Latin music, the bass plays rhythmic patterns that interact with percussion, often using syncopated and repetitive lines that emphasize the clave rhythm. It provides the heartbeat of genres like salsa, bossa nova, and samba.

Reggae: The bass in reggae plays a dominant role, using deep, repetitive lines that define the song's groove. It often emphasizes the "off-beats" and works closely with the drums to create a laid-back, relaxed feel, as seen in the works of **Aston "Family Man" Barrett (Bob Marley & The Wailers).**

UPRIGHT BASS

Upright players generally approach their instrument differently than the bass guitar:

Bowing (Arco): In bowing, the player uses a bow to draw sound from the strings. Two primary types of bows are used: the French bow (held like a violin bow) and the German bow (held with an underhand grip). Bowing produces a sustained, resonant sound that can range from soft and lyrical to loud and powerful, depending on the pressure and speed of the bow. Bowing is typically used in classical music, where the bass often provides long, sustained notes that underpin harmonic progressions. It is also used in orchestral and chamber music for expressive playing and melodic lines.

Pizzicato: The player plucks the strings with their fingers, producing a more percussive and staccato sound than bowing. This technique is commonly used in jazz, bluegrass, and other non-classical genres. In jazz, for instance, pizzicato often gives the bass its characteristic walking or swinging feel. A bassist uses a different approach when playing jazz vs. classical. A jazz player will use the side of the finger to create a full tone. A classical player plucks with more precision, aiming for a clearer, more focused sound.

Slap Bass: Slap bass is a percussive playing technique that combines striking and snapping the strings to produce a distinctive, rhythmic sound characterized by sharp, popping tones and deep, punchy thumps. This method involves two primary actions: **slapping** and **popping**. The slapping motion is performed by striking the string with the side or pad of the thumb near the base of the neck, causing the string to rebound off the fretboard and create a robust, percussive note. Popping is achieved by hooking a finger (usually the index or middle finger) underneath a string and pulling it away from the fretboard before releasing it, allowing the string to snap back against the frets and emitting a bright, snappy sound. Slap bass often incorporates hammer-ons, pull-offs, and left-hand muting techniques to add complexity and groove. This style is prevalent in genres like funk, disco, and certain forms of rock and jazz, and it requires precise timing, coordination, and control to execute effectively.

Thumb Position: In higher registers, bassists use thumb position, a technique in which the thumb is placed on the fingerboard to serve as a fret or stop while the other fingers press the strings. This technique is often used in classical and solo jazz performances to access higher notes and maintain control over the instrument's range.

UPRIGHT BASS: ROLE IN DIFFERENT GENRES

Classical Music: The upright bass provides the harmonic foundation and supports the orchestra with deep, resonant tones. It is often used to sustain long notes in the lower register, adding depth to the ensemble's overall sound. In symphonic and chamber music, bassists blend with string instruments with the bow (arco). In solo and concerto settings, the bass can also take on more melodic roles, showcasing its full range of expression.

Jazz: In jazz, the upright bass typically plays pizzicato, which outlines chord progressions through walking bass lines, a signature rhythmic element in swing and bebop styles. Jazz bassists like Ray Brown and Charles Mingus helped define the role of the upright bass as both a rhythmic and harmonic anchor. While pizzicato is the primary technique, bowing can also be used in more avant-garde or free jazz contexts for expressive solos or dramatic effects. Jazz bassists use pizzicato to create a robust and rhythmic pulse, often in interaction with the drums.

Bluegrass: The upright bass plays a vital rhythmic role in bluegrass, providing a steady "boom-chick" feel that drives the ensemble forward.
Players typically use pizzicato, and slap bass is prevalent, where the snapping of the strings adds a rhythmic, percussive element that complements the banjo, guitar, and fiddle. Unlike jazz, where the bass walks through chord changes, bluegrass bassists often play the more straightforward root and fifth patterns, maintaining a solid groove that supports the band.

Blues and Rockabilly: In blues and rockabilly, slap bass creates a driving, energetic rhythm that complements the fast, upbeat tempo of the music. This percussive technique adds a dynamic, lively element to the music and is often a hallmark of the genre's sound.

Latin Music: In Latin genres such as salsa and tango, the upright bass plays a rhythmic and harmonic role, often using syncopated bass lines to interact with the complex percussion patterns. Players frequently switch between pizzicato and arco, depending on the mood and structure of the piece.

CONTRABASS

The contrabass and upright bass are virtually the same instrument, the double bass. Larger sizes are more prevalent in symphonies due to the more resonant quality they provide. However, there are differences in playing techniques and applications, particularly in classical or symphonic settings:

Tuning and Size: While the standard upright bass is tuned in fourths (E-A-D-G), the contrabass can sometimes have an extension on the E string or even be fitted with five strings (adding a low C or B string), allowing it to reach lower notes, which is particularly useful in symphonic works.

Due to these extensions or additional strings, playing the contrabass can require adjustments in left-hand technique, as musicians must stretch further or use different fingering to access the extended range.

Bowing Techniques: In orchestral settings, the contrabass is primarily played with a bow (arco) and provides deep, rich, resonant tones that support harmony. Advanced bowing techniques such as **legato**, **spiccato** (bouncing the bow off the string), and **col legno** (using the bow's wood) are more commonly employed to match the articulation and dynamics required in symphonic music. The contrabass also extensively uses vibrato, subtle glissandi (sliding between notes), and more complex bowing styles to blend seamlessly with the lower strings (cello and viola sections) and provide a cohesive orchestral texture.

Pizzicato: While the pizzicato technique (plucking strings) is used in both upright bass and contrabass, in the symphonic context, pizzicato on the contrabass tends to be more deliberate and sustained, often providing a percussive, resonant effect that complements the overall orchestral sound.

ROLE OF CONTRABASS IN SYMPHONIES

The contrabass adds depth and power to the string section in a symphony orchestra. It often performs the following functions:

Harmonic Foundation: The contrabass, with its ability to provide the lowest notes in the string section, is the cornerstone of the orchestra's harmonic structure. Its rich, deep tones not only anchor the harmony but also reinforce the bass lines, ensuring the orchestral sound is full and resonant, a testament to the instrument's indispensability in the symphonic orchestra.

Doubling the Cello Section: The contrabass frequently doubles the cello part, an octave lower, enriching the orchestra's sound with a fuller, richer texture. This doubling not only enhances the weight and warmth of the music but also adds to the sense of depth, ensuring that the lower frequencies are well represented, and the orchestra's sound is rich and full.

Rhythmic Support: In symphonic works, the contrabass is a key player in establishing the rhythmic pulse, particularly in fast, energetic passages. Its rhythmic precision not only contributes to the overall timing but also adds to the drive and energy of the orchestra, particularly in movements with strong, driving rhythms, making the audience feel the instrument's contribution to the orchestra's energy and drive.

Melodic Passages: While less common, there are moments when the contrabass takes on a more melodic role, especially in modern and contemporary symphonic compositions. These passages showcase the instrument's ability to play more lyrically and provide a contrast to its typical supporting role.

Now that I've described the bass, let's start learning how to play. The most important thing you can do when learning is to stay focused and not get distracted or disappointed by sometimes slow progress. Everyone starts at the same point, and you succeed when you put your heart and soul into the process. My friend, multi-platinum recording artist **Rod Stewart,** said:

"You've got to have this burning desire in your chest to succeed."

Tad Sisler with Rod Stewart
Source – Sisler Private Collection

SECTION TWO
GENRES AND PLAYING STYLES

ROCK AND POP BASSLINES

In rock and pop music, the bass guitar plays a foundational role, creating rhythm and groove, anchoring the harmony, and driving the song's energy. The bass lines in these genres, whether simple or complex, are a testament to the instrument's significance in shaping the overall sound and feel of a song.

Root Note Playing: One of the most common techniques in rock and pop bass playing is focusing on the root notes of the chords. The bassist plays the main note of each chord, providing a solid foundation for the rest of the band. This simple but effective approach allows the song's rhythm and harmony to shine without overpowering the other instruments. It's prevalent in early rock, punk, and straightforward pop tracks.

Driving Eighth Notes: A defining characteristic of many rock and pop bass lines is steady, driving eighth notes. This technique involves playing the same note repeatedly in a rhythmic, pulsating manner, which helps create a sense of urgency and momentum. It's often heard in genres like hard rock, pop-rock, and classic rock, as demonstrated by bands like **AC/DC** and **The Ramones.**

Melodic Bass Lines: In some rock and pop songs, the bass plays a more melodic role, adding intricate lines that complement the main melody. This style is typical in bands where the bass is given a more prominent position, such as in **The Beatles,** where **Paul McCartney's** bass lines often served as a secondary melody, or in funk-influenced rock bands like **Red Hot Chili Peppers,** where **Flea's** playing adds a melodic groove.

"Anything worth doing good takes a little chaos."
— Michael "Flea" Balzary

Flea

Credit — Wikimedia Commons

Slap and Pop Techniques: In funk-infused rock and pop, slap and pop techniques create a percussive, punchy sound. This method, popularized by players like **Flea** and **Mark King,** involves slapping the strings with the thumb and popping them with the fingers, adding a rhythmic, danceable element to the bass line.

Chordal Bass Playing: Although less common, some rock and pop bassists use chords to create fuller, harmonic textures. This technique, used by players like **Geddy Lee (Rush),** adds a richer harmonic dimension to the bass parts.

JAZZ TECHINQUES FOR UPRIGHT BASS

In jazz, particularly in songs that swing, the upright bass is often played using walking bass lines. You play a continuous, flowing line of quarter notes that "walk" through the chords in a forward motion. This technique is fundamental to jazz and requires a strong sense of rhythm, harmony, and improvisation.

Walking Bass Technique: The walking bass involves playing a steady stream of quarter notes that outline a song's chord changes. The bassist typically starts with the chord's root note but moves to other chord tones (3rds, 5ths, 7ths) and passing notes to create a smooth, linear progression. This movement gives the music its characteristic swing and helps maintain the piece's harmonic structure.

Approach Notes and Chromaticism: Jazz bassists often use approach notes—notes that lead into the next chord tone—to create smooth transitions between chords. These can be chromatic (moving by half steps) or diatonic (staying within the scale), adding a sense of tension and release to the bass line. This technique gives jazz bass lines their fluid and unpredictable feel.

Syncopation and Rhythmic Variation: Unlike rock bass lines, which have a strict eighth-note feel, jazz walking bass lines incorporate syncopation and rhythmic variation, emphasizing off-beats or unexpected rhythmic accents. This makes the lines feel more spontaneous and dynamic, contributing to the swing or bebop feel.

Use of Arpeggios and Scales: Walking bass lines often incorporate arpeggios (playing the individual notes of a chord) and scales to create a logical, musical flow through the chord progressions. Jazz bassists blend major, minor, diminished, and dominant arpeggios with scalar passages to add depth and complexity to their lines.

Double Stops and Chords: Advanced jazz bassists may use double stops (playing two notes simultaneously) or even full chords to add harmonic richness to their lines. This is more common in solo sections or smaller ensembles where the bassist has more freedom to experiment.

TECHNIQUES FOR CONTRABASS

In classical music, the contrabass plays a vital role in the orchestra's string section, providing depth, weight, and harmonic support. Its playing style primarily focuses on bowing techniques (arco), although pizzicato is occasionally used for special effects.

Bowing (Arco) Technique: In classical music, the contrabass is most often played with a bow, which allows for sustained, resonant tones. This technique helps blend the contrabass with the rest of the string section, creating a cohesive, unified sound. Bowing techniques in classical music can range from smooth, sustained legato playing to more articulated staccato or spiccato (bouncing bow) strokes, depending on the passage and the desired effect.

Harmonic Foundation: In an orchestra, the contrabass often doubles the cello part an octave lower, reinforcing the bass line and providing a solid harmonic foundation. This doubling helps create a richer sound and ensures the lower frequencies are well represented, anchoring the entire orchestra.

Rhythmic and Dynamic Support: The contrabass contributes to the rhythmic drive of the orchestra, especially in more energetic, dramatic passages. It often plays simple parts that outline the harmonic progression rhythmically, allowing the higher strings, brass, and woodwinds to carry the main melodic content. However, the contrabass can also contribute to dynamic contrasts, playing with varying degrees of intensity to enhance the emotional impact of a piece.

Pizzicato: While primarily used in bowed passages, the contrabass occasionally plays pizzicato in classical music, where the strings are plucked with the fingers. This technique produces a more percussive, resonant sound and is often used in rhythmic, dance-like sections or to create special effects, such as in **Gustav Holst's** *"The Planets."*

Solo Passages and Virtuosity: Although rare, there are moments when the contrabass takes on a solo role in orchestral music. In these instances, the bass may employ more advanced techniques like harmonics (playing overtones by lightly touching the string), vibrato (a slight oscillation in pitch), and thumb position (using the thumb on the fingerboard to access higher notes). Such solos showcase the instrument's range and versatility, as heard in concertos and works by composers like **Serge Koussevitzky** and **Giovanni Bottesini.**

No matter what you play, play it with passion. My old friend, legendary multi-platinum artist **Kenny Rogers** said:

"I've always said music should make you laugh, make you cry or make you think. Don't be afraid to give up the good for the great."

Tad Sisler and Family with Kenny Rogers
Source – Sisler Private Collection

SECTION THREE
CORE TECHNIQUES ACROSS ALL BASSES

Bass instruments share fundamental techniques for producing a clear, controlled, and powerful sound. Here's a detailed look, including plucking vs. bowing, finger placement, and posture differences:

PLUCKING VS. BOWING

Plucking (Pizzicato): Plucking, or pizzicato, is the technique of playing bass strings by pulling or plucking them with the fingers. It's the dominant technique for electric bass guitar, and many bassists use it in jazz, rock, pop, blues, bluegrass, and many contemporary genres. It is also occasionally used in classical and orchestral settings for double bass.

Players use their index and middle fingers alternately to pluck the strings on the electric **bass guitar**, providing a smooth, even tone. Use a pick (plectrum) for a more aggressive sound.

On the **upright bass**, pizzicato involves pulling the string with the side of the index or middle finger, creating a resonant, warm tone. Jazz bassists often use a faster, more rhythmic plucking technique to create walking bass lines.

Bowing (Arco): Bowing is a technique unique to the upright bass and contrabass. It is commonly used in classical music, some jazz compositions, and orchestral playing. It produces sustained, rich tones, allowing for greater dynamic and tonal control. Bowing involves drawing a horsehair bow across the strings using a **French bow** (overhand grip) or a **German bow** (underhand grip). The bowing technique requires precise control of pressure, speed, and angle to produce different articulations, such as legato (smooth), staccato (short and detached), and spiccato (bouncing the bow).

WHEN TO USE THESE TECHNIQUES:

Plucking is used when a more rhythmic, percusive, or groovy feel is desired, fitting genres like rock, pop, jazz, and bluegrass.

Bowing is ideal for orchestral and classical music, where long, sustained notes and dynamic variations are necessary. It provides a rich, resonant tone that blends with the string section.

FINGER PLACEMENT

Electric Bass Guitar: Proper finger placement is essential for both fretting and plucking. Players should press down on the strings just behind the fret to ensure a clean, buzz-free sound when fretting. The thumb should rest behind the neck to provide support and allow for efficient finger movement. The plucking hand should maintain relaxed, alternating movements between the index and middle fingers to achieve smooth, even tones. This ensures consistency in volume and attack across notes.

Upright Bass / Contrabass: Correct finger placement is even more critical due to the larger size and longer fingerboard. The left-hand fingers must press down with more strength, and players often use a technique called "1-2-4" fingering: The primary fingers used are I (index), 2 (middle), and 4 (pinky). The ring finger is often paired with the pinky to add strength, as the spacing between notes is wider. The thumb should rest behind the neck or even help press down on higher notes in the "thumb position," a technique used for playing in higher registers.

WHY CORRECT FINGER PLACEMENT MATTERS:

Intonation: Proper finger positioning ensures accurate pitch, crucial for playing in tune, especially on fretless instruments like the upright bass.

Efficiency and Speed: Correct placement minimizes unnecessary movement, allowing players to navigate the fingerboard quickly and accurately.

Injury Prevention: Maintaining proper finger placement reduces the risk of strain and injury, allowing for longer, pain-free playing sessions.

IMPORTANCE OF POSTURE AND DIFFERENCES
Electric Bass Guitar:

Sitting: When sitting, the bass should rest on the right thigh (for right-handed players) with the neck angled slightly upward. The back should remain straight, and the shoulders should be relaxed.

Standing: When standing, the bass should be adjusted using a strap to sit comfortably, with the neck angled slightly upward. The bass should hang in a way that allows easy access to the entire fretboard without excessive wrist bending. A common mistake is wearing the bass too low, which can strain the wrist and make playing difficult.

Upright Bass / Contrabass: The player stands or uses a tall stool, with the bass leaning slightly into their body.

The endpin (the adjustable spike at the bottom) should be set so that the nut (where the fingerboard meets the neck) is roughly at the player's forehead or eyebrow level. The left arm should remain relaxed, with the fingers curved naturally, while the right arm moves fluidly when using the bow or plucking strings. Maintain an upright posture with relaxed shoulders and arms, as improper posture can lead to fatigue or injury.

WHY PROPER POSTURE MATTERS
Comfort and Endurance: Proper posture reduces muscle tension and fatigue, allowing longer playing sessions without discomfort.

Technique and Sound Quality: Good posture enables more precise movements, leading to cleaner, more controlled playing and a better tone.

Injury Prevention: Poor posture can cause strain or repetitive stress injuries over time, especially in the wrists, shoulders, and back.

Building up finger dexterity and strength is as important as proper finger placement and posture, if you want to become a proficient bass player. Just like an athlete builds up endurance to excel at their sport, a great bassist strengthens his or her hands and trains them to be nimble and fast.

I learned early on to surround myself with musicians who were better than me so I could push myself and improve quickly while learning from the best. As my father always said, *"Your reach should always exceed your grasp."*

This was exemplified by my friend, the multi-platinum artist **Glen Campbell**. He was not only a successful singer but also an exceptional guitarist who played on numerous hit songs for other singers.

Before he had his own hit song, he became a first call recording artist with the famous **"Wrecking Crew"** of studio musicians in the 1960s. **Glen** famously said:

"I got to play with the big guys, the Wrecking Crew. They just blew me away. I learned a lot of stuff from those guys."

Mentorship and exposure to superior talent is what will propel you forward. Listen and learn from the masters. Always remember to push your boundaries, and a great place to start is by building finger dexterity and strength.

Glen Campbell Performing with Tad Sisler
Source- Sisler Private Collection

CHAPTER TWO
BUILDING FINGER DEXTERITY AND STRENGTH
ARTIST SPOTLIGHT
JACO PASTORIUS

J**aco Pastorius** is widely regarded as one of the greatest bassists of all time. Believe it or not, he faced difficulties with finger dexterity, partly because he initially started as a drummer. **Jaco** struggled with finger strength when transitioning to bass, especially when attempting to play complex lines. He overcame it by dedicating hours daily to extensive practice, working on challenging jazz standards, and using chromatic scale exercises and arpeggios to help increase his finger speed, fluidity, and independence. Relentless practice enabled **Jaco** to master complex finger techniques, including his famous "harmonics" and rapid runs, enabling him to have a successful career performing and recording with **Weather Report, Joni Mitchell,** and **Pat Matheny,** among others. **Jaco** talked about his practice in terms of miles on a car at one point when he said:

"I've been playing the bass guitar for almost twelve years and fretless for about nine, so I've got quite a bit of mileage in my hands already."

Persistence and practice will allow you to succeed at anything you do, as it did with **Jaco Pastorius** on his journey to mastery.

Jaco Pastorius
Credit – Brian McMillen, Wikimedia Commons

SECTION ONE: WARM-UP TECHNIQUES

Warming up helps prevent injury, increases finger dexterity, helps you become a fluid, controlled player, and reduces the risk of injury. Here are some techniques for warm-up:

FINGER AND HAND STRETCHES

Finger and hand stretches loosen up muscles, tendons, and joints, helping prevent strain and injury, especially for bassists who use repetitive finger movements.

Finger Spread Stretch: Start with your hand relaxed, then spread your fingers as wide as possible. Hold this position for about 10 seconds, and then relax. Repeat this stretch a few times to improve finger flexibility.

Finger Pull Stretch: Gently pull each finger back towards your wrist one at a time, holding each for about 5-10 seconds. This movement helps stretch the muscles and tendons in your fingers.

Wrist Flexor and Extensor Stretches:
•To stretch the wrist flexors, face your palm up and extend one arm in front of you. Pull back gently on your fingers with your other hand.
•For the wrist extensors, do the same but with your palm facing down.

Finger Rolls: With both hands, roll your fingers one at a time. Start with your index finger and move to the pinky, then reverse the order. This exercise helps loosen up the joints and improves overall finger mobility.

PLAYING SCALES

Playing scales is a fundamental part of warming up, helping you work on developing finger strength, dexterity, and familiarity with the fretboard.

Chromatic Scale:
•Begin at the first fret of your low E string (4th string) and play each note in sequence, moving up one fret at a time (e.g., F, F#, G, G#, etc.) until you reach the 12th fret, then descend back down. Use all four fingers, one per fret, to ensure that each finger is engaged.

•Practice this on all four strings, moving across the fretboard. This exercise strengthens finger independence and improves accuracy.

Major Scale:

•Start with a C major scale (C, D, E, F, G, A, B, C). Play the scale slowly and evenly, using proper fingering and staying relaxed.

•Practice in different positions and keys to become familiar with the entire fretboard. Start slowly, then gradually increase your speed as your fingers warm up and gain fluidity.

Pentatonic scales, both major and minor, are five-note scales widely used in genres like rock, blues, and jazz due to their versatile and consonant sound.

Understanding **modes** expands a bassist's ability to navigate different tonal landscapes. Modes are scales derived from the major scale but starting on different degrees, resulting in unique interval patterns.

The seven modes—Ionian, Dorian, Phrygian, Lydian, Mixolydian, Aeolian, and Locrian—each have distinct characteristics. For example, the **Dorian mode** (natural minor with a raised sixth) is prevalent in jazz and funk, while the **Mixolydian mode** (major scale with a lowered seventh) is standard in blues and rock. Mastery of modes allows bassists to craft bass lines that enhance the modal qualities of a piece.

Applying scales and modes in bass plays involves creating lines that outline the underlying harmony while adding melodic interest. When improvising or composing, bassists can use scale tones to construct bass lines that fit seamlessly within the harmonic context. For instance, using the **Mixolydian mode** over dominant seventh chords can emphasize the bluesy feel of a progression. Similarly, the **Dorian mode** can add a soulful touch to minor key songs.

Chord structures are another vital aspect of music theory for bassists. Understanding how chords are built from scales—by stacking thirds—enables bassists to anticipate chord changes and construct bass lines that complement the harmony. **Triads** (three-note chords) consist of the root, third, and fifth, forming the basic chords in music. Extending beyond triads, **seventh chords** add another layer of depth by including the seventh degree, essential in jazz and other complex genres.

Arpeggios are notes of a chord played sequentially rather than simultaneously. Arpeggios are indispensable for bassists to outline chord changes and add harmonic richness to bass lines. Practicing arpeggios helps internalize chord tones, crucial when walking bass lines or improvising solos. By targeting chord tones on strong beats, bassists reinforce the harmonic foundation of a piece.

Harmony is the interplay of different notes and chords in music. The bassist's role in harmony is foundational; they bridge the rhythmic and harmonic elements by providing the root motion that defines chord progressions.

Bass line construction involves creating patterns that support the chords played by harmonic instruments like guitars or keyboards. Effective bass lines often emphasize the root note but incorporate chord tones and passing notes for movement and interest.

Creating walking bass lines is a common practice in jazz and blues. This technique involves smoothly moving from one chord to the next using scale tones, arpeggios, and chromatic approaches. Walking bass lines provide a sense of forward motion and keep the harmonic rhythm engaging. Bassists must be adept at voice leading, connecting chord tones in a way that creates smooth transitions and logical movement between chords.

Voice leading moves individual musical lines or voices from one note to the next with minimal movement, creating a cohesive harmonic progression. For bassists, this means choosing notes that are close to each other when moving between chords, which results in bass lines that are melodically satisfying and harmonically supportive. Good voice leading enhances the overall musicality of a piece and makes the bass line more engaging.

Combining knowledge of scales, modes, chords, and harmony enables bassists to craft bass lines that are both supportive and expressive. It allows creative freedom while keeping the bass anchored to the song's structure. Whether playing a simple groove or a complex solo, this theoretical understanding ensures that every note serves the music effectively.

TIPS FOR PRACTICING SCALES

•Use a metronome to maintain consistent timing.
•Focus on using alternate plucking with your index and middle fingers (or a pick if you use one) to develop evenness and control.
•Vary your dynamics (play softly, then loudly) to improve your touch and control over the instrument.

RHYTHMIC WARM-UPS

Rhythmic warm-ups develop timing, groove, and finger coordination.

Basic Rhythmic Exercises:
•**Quarter Notes:** Play a simple note (e.g., the open E string) and a metronome, hitting each beat evenly. Start at a slow tempo (60-80 BPM) and gradually increase the speed.
•**Eighth Notes:** Play two notes per beat, maintaining an even rhythm. Focus on alternating between your index and middle fingers (or up and down strokes if using a pick).
•**Triplets:** Play three notes per beat to develop a sense of swing and coordination. This exercise is beneficial for jazz, funk, and blues styles.
•**Sixteenth Notes:** Play four notes per beat, ensuring that each note is even and consistent. This exercise will improve your finger speed and coordination.

•**Syncopated Rhythms:** Practice playing off-beat and syncopated patterns, such as "1 & 2 & 3 & 4 &" while only plucking on the "&" counts. This exercise improves your ability to handle complex rhythms and develop a sense of groove.

•**Walking Basslines:** Create simple walking basslines using the major scale or arpeggios, focusing on staying in time with the metronome. Gradually increase the complexity by incorporating chromatic passing notes, arpeggios, and different rhythmic patterns.

TIPS FOR EFFECTIVE WARM-UPS

Start Slow: Begin your warm-up at a comfortable, slow tempo to ensure accuracy and prevent strain. Gradually increase the speed as your fingers warm up and become more agile.

Maintain Good Posture: Keep your wrist straight, your shoulders relaxed and avoid tension in your hands and arms. Proper posture helps you avoid injury and improves playing efficiency.

Use a Metronome: Bassists should always practice with a metronome to develop consistent timing and rhythm, which are essential skills.

Warm Up Both Hands: During your warm-up routine, ensure that both your fretting and plucking hands are engaged. This action helps balance finger strength and coordination.

My dear friend **Marshall Hawkins** is considered one of the outstanding upright bassists of our time. As a mentor, he emphasizes the need for dexterity and strength. **Marshall** performed with **Miles Davis, Shirley Horn,** and many others, later becoming a beloved mentor, working with the *Idyllwild Arts Foundation* in Idyllwild, CA. **Marshall** and I recorded in my studio on an outstanding original project entitled **"Jazz Masters: The Barcelona Sessions"** with a handful of the best performers alive, including **Marty Morell,** legendary **Bill Evans** drummer. **Marshall** said:

"Without music, life would Bb!"

**Marty Morell and Marshall Hawkins
in Tad Sisler's Studio**
Source – Sisler Private Collection

SECTION TWO
STRENGTH-BUILDING EXERCISES

Building finger strength enables better control, precision, and endurance.

CHROMATIC DRILLS help you develop finger strength, independence, and dexterity across the fretboard. They involve playing notes in a step-by-step sequence, engaging all four fingers.

Basic Chromatic Exercise: Start on the 1st fret of the low E string with your index finger and play one note per fret: 1st (index), 2nd (middle), 3rd (ring), and 4th (pinky).
Continue this sequence up the string (e.g., F, F#, G, G#), then move to the next string and repeat the pattern. After reaching the highest string, descend back down the fretboard using the same pattern. Ensure that each finger remains close to the fretboard and that you use alternate plucking (index and middle fingers) or a consistent picking pattern.
•**Variation 1:** Start at the 5th fret and move up and down the fretboard chromatically, using all four fingers and shifting positions. This exercise helps build finger strength and muscle memory across a broader range.
•**Variation 2 (Stretch Drill):** Play the same chromatic pattern, leaving each finger in place until all four fingers are down on the frets. This exercise increases finger stretching ability and strength, especially in the pinky.
Benefits: It improves finger independence and strength, allowing for smoother, more precise playing. It also enhances muscle memory, enabling quick transitions between frets.

STRING SKIPPING EXERCISES

String skipping exercises help strengthen finger coordination and agility while improving control over jumps between non-adjacent strings. This technique is beneficial for playing more complex bass lines and melodies.

Basic String Skipping Exercise: Start on the low E string, fretting a note (e.g., 3rd fret with your index finger), then pluck the note. Skip the A string and move to the D string, playing a note on the same fret (3rd fret). Continue this pattern across the fretboard (e.g., G string, then back to D string, skipping strings each time). Use alternate plucking or a pick to focus on clean transitions and maintain consistent timing.

Extended String Skipping Drill: Play a chromatic pattern on one string (e.g., 1st to 4th frets on the E string), then skip to the D string and repeat the pattern. Reverse the exercise, moving up and down the strings, alternating between skipping one and two strings.

Benefits: It develops finger strength and control, as string skipping requires more power and precision than playing on adjacent strings.

It improves right-hand (plucking or picking) accuracy and coordination, crucial for complex bass lines.

BOW PRESSURE EXERCISES
(For Upright Bass/Contrabass Players)

For upright bass and contrabass players, bow pressure exercises help you develop strength, control, and consistency in bowing, leading to a fuller, more dynamic sound.

Sustained Long Tones: Choose an open string (e.g., G string) and draw the bow slowly across it, applying even pressure from the frog to the tip (the entire length of the bow).

Maintain a steady tone and consistent volume, focusing on producing a rich, resonant sound. Gradually increase the pressure without causing the bow to bounce or create scratchy sounds, strengthening the arm and fingers.

Dynamic Bowing Exercise: Start with light bow pressure at the frog, gradually increasing pressure as you move toward the tip and then decreasing pressure on your way back. This exercise builds strength and teaches control over varying dynamics, allowing you to produce more expressive, nuanced tones.

Spiccato Bowing (Bouncing Bow): Practice a spiccato bowing technique by allowing the bow to bounce lightly off the strings, using small, controlled movements. Start with a slower tempo, ensuring each bounce is consistent, then gradually increase speed. This exercise strengthens your wrist, forearm, and fingers while improving bow control.

Benefits: It builds arm, hand, and finger strength, essential for sustaining clear, strong tones with the bow. Improves dynamic control, allowing for better articulation and expression in bowing.

Learning is not supposed to always be easy. You will experience moments of deep frustration, especially at first. Stay focused and understand that painful moments are necessary to master any worthy endeavor. Be brave. My friend, legendary actress **Mary Tyler Moore** said:

"You can't be brave if you've only had wonderful things happen to you."

Tad Sisler and Mary Tyler Moore
Source – Sisler Private Collection

ADDITIONAL STRENGTH-BUILDING TIPS

Finger Rolling Exercise: Place all four fingers on the same fret across four adjacent strings (e.g., 5th fret on E, A, D, G strings). Roll each finger individually to press down and pluck each string in sequence, then reverse the order. This exercise helps strengthen finger muscles and promotes finger independence.

Spider Exercise: Position your fingers on the 1st to 4th frets of the E string and play them in sequence (1-2-3-4). Then move to the A string but reverse the pattern (4-3-2-1). Continue up and down the fretboard, alternating the pattern on each string. This challenging exercise develops finger strength, independence, and coordination.

Resistance Training: Use a rubber band or grip trainer to build finger strength. Stretch the rubber band around your fingers and repeatedly open and close your hand. This exercise is excellent for strengthening the smaller muscles for fretting and plucking.

TIPS FOR EFFECTIVE STRENGTH-BUILDING

Start Slow: Always begin at a comfortable pace, ensuring proper finger placement and control before increasing speed. This action prevents bad habits and injuries.

Consistency: To build and maintain finger strength, practice these exercises daily, even for just 10-15 minutes.

Use a Metronome: Maintain steady timing while practicing these exercises, which enhances your rhythmic accuracy.

Stay Relaxed: Avoid excessive tension in your hands, wrists, and shoulders. Proper technique ensures that your muscles strengthen without strain.

BOOKS FOR LEARNING AND ONLINE TUTORIALS

I structured this book as a road map for anyone to learn how to become a master at playing bass. I will give you a crash course on music theory and harmony, but you must bury yourself in technique to become a great player. I've listed some great resources here, but I do not endorse, nor do I have any financial interest in, any of these resources:

"Hal Leonard Bass Method" by Ed Friedland is one of the most comprehensive and beginner-friendly bass learning books. This method covers the fundamentals of bass playing, including reading music, scales, and different techniques. Beginners widely use it, and it provides a solid foundation for all styles of bass playing.

"Bass Guitar for Dummies" by Patrick Pfeiffer: Part of the *"For Dummies"* series, this book is perfect for beginners who want an easy-to-understand guide to bass guitar. It covers the basics, from finger placement and rhythm to more advanced concepts like slap bass and improvisation.

"The Complete Electric Bass Player" by Chuck Rainey: Chuck Rainey, a legendary bassist, has created this book series that takes you from beginner to advanced levels. It covers everything from basic techniques and finger exercises to complex rhythms, grooves, and playing in various styles.

"Building Walking Bass Lines" by Ed Friedland: Ideal for bassists who want to learn jazz and blues, this book focuses on constructing walking bass lines. It covers concepts such as chord tones, scale approaches, chromatic approaches, and more, helping players understand how to create melodic, flowing bass lines.

"Bass Fitness: An Exercising Handbook" by Josquin des Prés: My friend **Josquin** designed this book to improve finger strength, speed, and dexterity. It contains exercises and drills that challenge players at all levels, making it a great supplement to any bass player's practice routine. **Josquin** is a record producer, songwriter, and TV composer who worked with lyricist **Bernie Taupin** and platinum artist **Jason Mraz** on several compositions.

Josquin Des Pres, Tad Sisler,
and American Idol Top 10 Finalist Makayla Phillips
Source – Sisler Private Collection

ONLINE RESOURCES

Scott's Bass Lessons (scottsbasslessons.com): One of the most popular and comprehensive online bass learning platforms, **Scott's Bass Lessons** offers a vast library of video lessons, masterclasses, and courses taught by **Scott Devine** and other renowned bass players, covering beginner basics to advanced techniques across various genres.

TalkingBass (talkingbass.net): Created by professional bassist **Mark Smith**, *TalkingBass* offers structured courses, free video lessons, and resources for all levels. It covers topics like technique, scales, chords, and sight-reading, strongly emphasizing building a solid musical foundation.

BassBuzz (bassbuzz.com): *BassBuzz* is perfect for beginners and offers step-by-step video lessons that are easy to follow. The course *"Beginner to Badass"* is a popular and engaging program that takes learners from complete novices to competent bass players, focusing on fun and practical learning.

StudyBass (studybass.com): A free resource that provides detailed lessons on bass technique, theory, and song tutorials.
StudyBass is an excellent choice for self-learners who want to understand the fundamentals of bass playing and music theory without paying for a subscription.

YouTube Channels (e.g., Daric Bennett's Bass Lessons, Janek Gwizdala's Channel): *YouTube* has numerous high-quality bass lessons and tutorials. Channels like **Daric Bennett's** Bass Lessons and **Janek Gwizdala** offer free lessons on techniques, theory, and genre-specific playing. These channels are great for picking up tips and learning quickly.

> *"The obvious priority is to get your intonation together. Your sound and your pitch should be inspiring to people, not a distraction."*
> *– John Patitucci*

MUSIC COLLEGES/UNITED STATES:

Schools like the **Musicians Institute** in Hollywood, CA are completely acceptable. **MI** has an excellent vocal, drum, guitar, and audio engineering program. I have friends who work with headliner artists and compose for film and television who have graduated from **MI**. Here are some more prestigious schools of music education:

Juilliard School (New York, NY): **Juilliard** is renowned for its rigorous training and high standards, offering voice and opera performance degrees. Its alumni include **Renee Fleming, Nina Simone, Audra McDonald,** and **David Bryan.**

Berklee College of Music (Boston, MA): Known for its contemporary music programs, **Berklee offers** extensive vocal performance programs, including jazz and popular music. It has a diverse curriculum and notable alumni like **John Mayer** and **Esperanza Spalding.** This program has a high bar for qualification, so you should be excellent and prepared to be the best.

Curtis Institute of Music (Philadelphia, PA): **Curtis** is highly selective, admitting only a few students each year, and provides full-tuition scholarships to all its students. It focuses on classical and opera training with a strong emphasis on performance.

Indiana University Jacobs School of Music (Bloomington, IN): One of the largest music schools in the **United States, Jacobs** offers various programs and degrees in vocal performance. It has a notable faculty and alumni network, including **Joshua Bell** and **Leonard Slatkin.**

New England Conservatory of Music (Boston, MA): **NEC** offers comprehensive programs in voice and opera, with a strong emphasis on performance and musicianship. It is deeply integrated into **Boston's** vibrant music scene.

MUSIC COLLEGES/EUROPE:

Royal College of Music (London, UK): Founded in 1882, this institution is consistently ranked as one of the top music schools globally, offering a wide range of degrees in various musical disciplines and boasting top-notch facilities and a distinguished faculty.

Royal Conservatoire of Scotland (Glasgow, Scotland): Known for its excellent music, drama, and dance programs, the **Royal Conservatoire of Scotland** hosts over 500 public performances each year, providing ample performance opportunities for students.

Royal Academy of Music (London, UK): The oldest conservatoire in the **UK**, founded in 1822, the **Royal Academy of Music** offers a range of programs from Bachelor's Degrees to advanced diplomas. It has a rich history of producing celebrated musicians such as **Elton John** and **Annie Lennox**.

Conservatoire National Supérieur de Musique et de Danse de Paris (CNSMDP) (Paris, France): Established in 1795, **CNSMDP** is one of **Europe's** leading institutions for music and dance, with comprehensive programs in musical disciplines.

Universität für Musik und darstellende Kunst Wien (Vienna, Austria): Located in **Vienna**, a city renowned for its classical music heritage, this university offers many music degrees. It is one of the largest and most prestigious music schools in **Europe.**

Whatever you do, continually expand your horizons, and never stop learning. My biggest challenge in these times is keeping up with technological advances and staying current. Still, ultimately, making it all boils down to talent and persistence. My dear friend, iconic actor **Elliott Gould** believed strongly in persistence when he said:

"Quitters don't win, and winners don't quit."

Tad Sisler and Elliott Gould
Source – Sisler Private Collection

SECTION THREE
DEVELOPING SPEED AND ACCURACY

Focused practice, a solid understanding of timing, and developing control over different playing techniques will help you improve your speed and accuracy as a bassist. Here are some ideas to help:

METRONOME PRACTICE helps ensure that your timing is precise and your technique is consistent.

"So, first you have to be able to play with a metronome. Then you take your freedom. If you play in an orchestra, you got to watch the conductor, he is like a metronome, but it is more difficult because he can change rhythms." – Ruggiero Ricci

Ruggiero Ricci
Credit – Wikimedia Commons

Start Slow: Set the metronome at a comfortable, slow tempo (around 50-60 BPM). Play a simple exercise, scale, or bass line in time with each click. Focusing on playing each note clearly and evenly helps you develop accuracy and muscle memory.

Gradual Increase in Speed: Once you can play the exercise accurately at a slow tempo, gradually increase the metronome speed by 2-5 BPM. Continue this process, ensuring you maintain accuracy and control at each new tempo. This slow and steady approach allows your fingers to adapt and strengthens muscle memory, making it easier to play at higher speeds.

Subdividing Beats: Practice playing quarter notes, then eighth notes, triplets, and sixteenth notes at the same tempo to challenge your speed and accuracy. This exercise improves your consistent timing while transitioning between different note values.

Use Alternate Plucking or Picking: When practicing with a metronome, use alternate plucking with your index and middle fingers (or consistent up and down strokes if using a pick). This exercise helps you develop evenness in your playing and prevents fatigue.

Metronome practice reinforces consistent timing, helps you internalize rhythm, and gradually builds finger speed without sacrificing accuracy.

LEGATO AND STACCATO TECHNIQUES

Understanding and mastering **legato and staccato techniques** teaches you to control the length and articulation of each note.

Legato Technique: Legato means playing notes smoothly and connected, without any gaps between them. For bass players, this involves minimizing the space between finger movements and ensuring each note flows seamlessly into the next.

Hammer-ons and Pull-offs: These are core legato techniques. For a hammer-on, play a note, then "hammer" your finger onto the next fret without re-plucking. For a pull-off, pluck the first note and then "pull" the fretting finger off to let the next note ring. Practice playing scales or chromatic exercises using hammer-ons and pull-offs to develop smoothness and finger strength. This exercise will help you play faster while maintaining fluidity.

Staccato Technique: Staccato means playing notes sharply and detached, with a brief silence between each note. To achieve this on the bass, pluck the string and immediately lift your fretting finger slightly to mute the note, creating a short, crisp sound. Practice alternating between legato and staccato while playing scales or exercises. This action helps you develop control over your finger movements and teaches you to articulate notes clearly at any speed.

Developing legato and staccato techniques enhances finger control and articulation, allowing you to switch between smooth and sharp playing effortlessly.

COMPLEX RHYTHM PATTERNS

To be an accurate and versatile bassist, you must be comfortable with **complex rhythmic patterns**, syncopation, and rhythm shifts, common in genres like jazz, funk, and progressive rock.

Syncopation Practice: Syncopation involves playing notes off the beat or emphasizing weaker beats. Start by practicing simple bass lines with a metronome, then introduce syncopated rhythms by accenting off-beats (e.g., playing on the "and" of each beat instead of directly on the beat). One effective exercise is to play a steady stream of eighth notes but mute the notes on the downbeats and accent the off-beats. This will help you lock into complex rhythms and maintain a groove.

Rhythm Shifts: Practice shifting between different rhythmic subdivisions in the same exercise (e.g., switching between eighth, triplets, and sixteenth notes). Start with the metronome slowly and focus on staying in time as you transition between different note values.

You can also practice playing bass lines in odd time signatures (e.g., 5/4, 7/8) to challenge your sense of timing and improve your ability to adapt to unusual rhythmic patterns.

Polyrhythmic Exercises: Polyrhythms involve playing two different rhythmic patterns simultaneously (e.g., playing triplets with your fingers while tapping quarter notes with your foot). Start slowly with basic polyrhythmic patterns (e.g., 3 against 2) and gradually work up to more complex combinations.

Practicing complex rhythmic patterns and syncopation helps you develop a strong sense of timing, groove, and rhythmic accuracy, enabling you to adapt to new musical styles.

Equally as important are timing and rhythmic precision. In the next chapter, we will stress the importance of playing in the pocket, locking in with the drummer, and maintaining precision. Nobody knew better the importance of precision and focus than my friend, **General Colin Powell**, who became **United States Secretary of State**. **Powell** said:

"There are no secrets to success. It is the result of preparation, hard work, and learning from failure."

Secretary of State, General Colin Powell with Tad Sisler
Source – Sisler Private Collection

CHAPTER THREE
MASTERING TIMING AND RHYTHM

"Music deals with time and timing. It's so magical, but when you get into it, every little sound and every little space between the sounds, it's critical, so critical. And if it's not there, it not only feels wrong, but it ruins things.
– David Lynch

SECTION ONE
UNDERSTANDING RHYTHMIC NOTATION

Music is math. Theory and harmony provide the foundation for a greater understanding of music, just as Geometry does to architecture and Calculus to computer programming. The knowledge you gain provides a benchmark for critical thinking. You use it in more ways than you would ever imagine without knowing it! Mastering timing requires an understanding of notes, time signatures, and reading syncopation.

QUARTER NOTES (♩):
• Quarter notes are the basic unit of rhythm in most music. They receive one beat in 4/4 time and are represented by a filled-in note head with a straight stem.
• When playing quarter notes, you play one note per beat, evenly spaced. For example, if you're playing a bass line in 4/4 time, you would play four quarter notes per measure, with each note landing directly on each beat (1, 2, 3, 4). Use alternate plucking with your index and middle fingers or consistent picking to maintain an even rhythm.

EIGHTH NOTES (♪):
• Eighth notes are represented by a filled-in note head with a stem and one flag. They are worth half a beat, so there are two eighth notes per beat. When two or more eighth notes appear together, they are often connected by a single beam.
• In 4/4 time, you would play eight eighth notes in one measure. Count them as "1 & 2 & 3 & 4 &," ensuring that you pluck or pick evenly on each count and the "and" (&). For evenness, maintain steady alternate finger plucking or picking.

SIXTEENTH NOTES (♬):
• Sixteenth notes have a filled-in note head, a stem, and two flags. When grouped together, they are connected by two beams. A sixteenth note equals a quarter of a beat, meaning four sixteenth notes per beat.
• In 4/4 time, you would play sixteen sixteenth notes in one measure, counted as "1 e & a 2 e & a 3 e & a 4 e & a." Practice slowly at first, ensuring that each note is evenly spaced, and gradually increase your speed while maintaining accuracy.

TIPS FOR PRACTICING
• Use a metronome to keep a steady tempo, starting slowly and gradually increasing your speed.
• Clap the rhythms before playing them on your bass to internalize the timing.

•Practice each note value separately and then combine them to build rhythmic versatility.

TIME SIGNATURES indicate amount of beats per measure and what type of note gets one beat. Understanding time signatures helps maintain rhythm and playing in sync with the band.
Common Time Signatures:
4/4 (Common Time): This is the most frequently used time signature in popular music; four beats per measure; the quarter note receives one beat. Bass lines in 4/4 time often emphasize the 1st and 3rd beats for rock or funk grooves but can also play on every beat or use syncopated rhythms.
3/4: Three beats per measure; quarter note receives one beat. This is the time signature commonly found in waltzes, folk, and some classical pieces. Bass lines in 3/4 time frequently emphasize the first beat, creating a "boom-chick-chick" feel.
2/4: Two beats per measure; quarter note receives one beat. This time signature is common in marches, polkas, and some punk rock. Play a strong, driving line on both beats.
6/8: Six beats per measure; eighth note receives one beat. This time signature creates a rolling, triplet-based feel, commonly found in blues, ballads, and some rock and Latin music. Bass lines in 6/8 often emphasize the first and fourth beats to match the groove.
Uncommon Time Signatures:
5/4: Five beats per measure; quarter note receives one beat. This time signature is less common but appears in pieces like **Dave Brubeck's** *"Take Five."* Bass lines in 5/4 often emphasize patterns like 3+2 or 2+3 to create a sense of rhythmic flow.
7/8: Seven beats per measure; eighth note receives one beat. It's often divided into smaller groups like 2+2+3 or 3+2+2. You need to be aware of these subdivisions to maintain the groove. It's important to count in your head as you play so you don't lose the beat. You get better at this with practice.

STANDARD NOTATION AND TABLATURE
Beyond just playing notes, understanding standard notation and tablature enables you to read, interpret, and communicate music effectively across various settings.

READING THE BASS CLEF AND UNDERSTANDING NOTATION
BASS CLEF READING:
Bass Clef (F Clef): The bass clef is the standard notation used for bass instruments. It indicates the pitch of notes on a staff where each line and space correspond to a specific note.

Note Identification: Familiarize yourself with the notes on the lines (G, B, D, F, A) and spaces (A, C, E, G) from bottom to top.

RHYTHMIC NOTATION:

Note Values: Understand whole notes, half notes, quarter notes, eighth notes, sixteenth notes, and their corresponding rests.

Time Signatures: Grasp common time signatures like 4/4, 3/4, and 6/8, which dictate the number of beats per measure and the note value that receives one beat.

Rhythmic Patterns: Practice reading and clapping out rhythms to internalize different rhythmic feels.

INTERPRETING AND WRITING TABLATURE

In Section Two of this chapter, I gave you many resources for learning and writing tablature, and for other skills outlined here.

UNDERSTANDING TABLATURE (Tab)

Visual Layout: Tablature uses horizontal lines representing the strings of the bass, with numbers indicating the fret to be played.

Advantages: Tablature is intuitive for finger placement and is especially helpful for those who don't read standard notation.

WRITING TABLATURE

Creating Your Own Tabs: Write down bass lines you've composed or transcribed to share with others or for personal reference.

Combining with Rhythm Notation: Enhance tabs by including rhythmic indicators above the numbers to convey timing.

SIGHT-READING SKILLS

IMPORTANCE OF SIGHT READING

Professional Versatility: Reading music at first sight is invaluable in studio sessions and ensembles and learning new repertoire quickly.

Musical Independence: Facilitates learning without relying solely on recordings or rote memorization.

TECHNIQUES TO IMPROVE SIGHT READING PROFICIENCY

Daily Practice: Incorporate sight-reading into your regular practice routine using method books or online resources.

Start Simple: Begin with easy pieces and progressively tackle more complex works.

Use a Metronome: Develop a steady tempo, resist the urge to stop for mistakes, and keep moving forward.

Preview the Piece: Scan for key signatures, time signatures, repeats, and difficult passages before playing.

TRANSCRIPTION EXERCISES
TRANSCRIBING BASS LINES FROM RECORDINGS

Active Listening: Choose songs you enjoy and listen attentively to the bass parts.

Writing It Down: Attempt to notate the bass line using standard notation or tablature.

Benefits: Enhances ear training, reinforces understanding of musical structures, and expands your repertoire.

SIGHT-READING AND MUSICAL LITERACY
NAVIGATING LEAD SHEETS AND CHARTS

Lead Sheets: Contain melody, chords, and sometimes lyrics. Use chord symbols to construct appropriate bass lines.

Charts: May include detailed arrangements with specific bass parts or cues.

UNDERSTANDING COMMON NOTATION

Ensemble Playing: Reading parts accurately is critical in orchestras, big bands, or pit orchestras where individual parts contribute to a larger arrangement.

Studio Sessions: Quick reading skills allow for efficient recording processes.

RHYTHM SECTION READING

Locking In: Read drum cues and rhythmic hits to synchronize with other rhythm section members.

Cue Recognition: Be aware of written cues for dynamics, style changes, or specific articulations.

ADDITIONAL PRACTICE MATERIALS AND RESOURCES

Method Books: Explore books like *"Bass Fretboard Basics"* or *"Sight-Reading for the Bass."*

Online Platforms: Websites and apps like *MusicTutor* or *SightReadingFactory* offer interactive exercises.

Ensemble Participation: Join bands, orchestras, or jam sessions to apply reading skills in real time.

DYNAMICS AND ARTICULATION
EXPRESSIVE TECHNIQUES

Using Dynamics: Employ variations in volume—from soft (piano) to loud (forte)—to add emotional depth.

Crescendo and Diminuendo: Gradually increasing or decreasing volume to build tension or release.

ARTICULATION METHODS

Legato: Play notes smoothly and connect them, minimizing the space between them.

Staccato: Short, detached notes that add a rhythmic punch.

Vibrato: A slight fluctuation in pitch to add warmth and expressiveness.

Ghost Notes: Muted notes that provide rhythmic interest without strong pitch presence. We will elaborate more on ghost notes.

PHRASING

Musical Sentences: Think of bass lines as sentences with clear beginnings and endings to convey a story.

Breathing Spaces: Incorporate rests and pauses to enhance musicality and prevent monotony.

Emphasis: Highlight important notes or beats to align with the song's emotional contour.

EAR TRAINING AND AURAL SKILLS

Developing strong ear training and aural skills enables you to recognize musical elements by ear, improvise effectively, and play confidently without relying solely on written music. The following sections delve into critical areas of ear training for bassists:

INTERVAL RECOGNITION
IDENTIFYING INTERVALS BY EAR

Intervals are the distance between two notes and form melody and harmony building blocks. For bassists, recognizing intervals by ear is crucial for:

Creating Melodic Bass Lines: Understanding intervals helps craft bass lines that add harmonic depth and complement the melody.

Improvisation: Identifying intervals allows for spontaneous musical ideas during solos or fills, adding to your musical intuition.

Communication with Other Musicians: Helps in quickly learning songs and responding to musical cues.

TECHNIQUES TO DEVELOP INTERVAL RECOGNITION
INTERVAL EAR TRAINING EXERCISES

Ascending and Descending Intervals: Practice recognizing intervals played both upwards and downwards.

Singing Intervals: Vocalizing intervals can reinforce your ability to hear and identify them.

Use Reference Songs: Associate common intervals with familiar melodies (e.g., a perfect fourth sounds like the beginning of "Here Comes the Bride").

Interval Identification Apps:

Utilize ear training apps that focus on interval recognition to practice regularly.

PRACTICAL APPLICATION

Transcribe Bass Lines: Listen to songs and try to determine the intervals between notes in the bass line.

Improvise Using Intervals: Practice creating bass lines by focusing on specific intervals to internalize their sound and feel.

CHORD QUALITY IDENTIFICATION
MAJOR, MINOR, DIMINISHED, AND AUGMENTED CHORDS

Understanding chord qualities by ear allows bassists to:

Outline Harmony Effectively: Choose appropriate notes that highlight the chord's character.

Adapt to Harmonic Changes: Quickly adjust playing during jams or when the music shifts unexpectedly.

Enhance Musical Interaction: Communicate and connect with other musicians through a shared understanding of harmony.

TECHNIQUES TO RECOGNIZE CHORD QUALITIES
CHORD EAR TRAINING:

Listening Exercises: Play or listen to different chords and identify their qualities.

Singing Arpeggios: Vocalizing the notes of chords helps internalize their sound.

FOCUSING ON TRIADS:

Major Triads: Bright and happy sound.

Minor Triads: Sad or somber tone.

Diminished Triads: Tense and unstable feel.

Augmented Triads: Unsettled and mysterious quality.

Practice with Recordings: Identify chord qualities in your favorite songs and note how they affect the mood.

PRACTICAL APPLICATION

Create Bass Lines Emphasizing Chord Tones: Use the root, third, and fifth to solidify the harmony.

Improve Soloing: Knowing chord qualities helps select notes that fit the underlying chords during solos.

PLAYING BY EAR

Playing by ear empowers bassists to:

Learn Music Quickly: Pick up songs during rehearsals or gigs without relying on sheet music.

Develop Musical Memory: Strengthen the ability to remember songs and chord progressions.

Enhance Creativity: Encourage improvisation and personal expression in your playing.

TECHNIQUES FOR LEARNING SONGS BY EAR
ACTIVE LISTENING
Focus on the Bass Line: Isolate and concentrate on the bass parts in recordings.
Listen Repeatedly: Multiple listens help internalize the structure and nuances.

BREAKING DOWN THE SONG
Section by Section: Learn the song in manageable parts (intro, verse, chorus).
Identify Repeating Patterns: Recognize riffs and progressions that recur.

USING YOUR INSTRUMENT TO EXPLORE
Match Pitches: Find the notes you hear on your bass.
Experiment with Rhythms: Replicate the rhythmic feel of the bass line.

RECORD YOURSELF
Playback and Compare: Listen to your rendition alongside the original to spot differences.

LEVERAGE TECHNOLOGY
Slow Down Software: Use apps to reduce the song's tempo without changing pitch for detailed study.
Loop Sections: Focus on challenging parts by looping them.
Use AI: Check out our suggestions for AI apps in this book.

PRACTICAL APPLICATION
Join Jam Sessions: Apply your skills in real-time musical settings.
Transcribe Entire Songs: Challenge yourself to learn all parts of a song by ear.

TIPS FOR PRACTICING
•Use a metronome set to different time signatures to familiarize yourself with the feel of each one.
•Practice clapping or tapping along to songs with uncommon time signatures to internalize the rhythm.

READING AND PLAYING SYNCOPATION
Syncopation is a technique where notes are played off the beat or in between beats, creating a sense of rhythmic tension and excitement. It's widely used in funk, jazz, and Latin music to add groove and complexity to bass lines.
Understanding Offbeats: In 4/4 time, the main beats are 1, 2, 3, and 4, while the offbeats are the "and" (&) counts in between. Syncopated rhythms emphasize these offbeats rather than the main beats. For example, instead of playing on "1, 2, 3, 4," a syncopated bass line might emphasize "1 & 2 & 3 & 4 &," creating a less predictable groove.
Tied Notes: Syncopation often involves tied notes, where a note is sustained across beats. This creates a sense of rhythmic displacement, as you're holding a note over where a new beat would typically start. Practice playing a note on

beat 1 and tying it to the "and" of beat 2, then plucking again on beat 3. This reinforces the feeling of syncopation.

Anticipation and Delayed Attacks: Syncopated bass lines often involve playing notes just before or after the beat. For example, playing a note on the "and" of beat 4 leading into the next measure creates a feeling of forward motion and rhythmic interest.

The most important thing you can do as a musician is to listen to as many players, performances, and tracks in as many styles as possible for inspiration and knowledge and to become a more rounded player. My friend, legendary broadcaster **Larry King,** said it best:

"I remind myself every morning: Nothing I say this day will teach me anything. So, if I'm going to learn, I must do it by listening."

Larry King with Tad Sisler
Source – Sisler Private Collection

EXAMPLES OF SYNCOPATED PATTERNS
Try playing a bass line in which you emphasize beats 1 and 3 but also add a note on the "and" of beats 2 and 4. This simple syncopated rhythm adds energy and variation to your playing.

Tips for Practicing Syncopation: Practice syncopated rhythms slowly with a metronome, ensuring you accurately hit the offbeats and tied notes. Listen to funk, jazz, and Latin music to hear how syncopation is used in actual bass lines and try playing along to internalize the groove.

CIRCLE OF FIFTHS
Take the time to learn music theory and harmony to become a more rounded player. Start with the circle of fifths. Learning this helps you with theory, key signatures, chord progressions, and scale patterns:

Key Signatures: The circle of fifths visually shows you the relationship between different key signatures, making identifying sharps and flats in any key easier, helping you adapt quickly to different songs and genres.

Chord Progressions: Many common chord progressions in music follow the circle of fifths, such as I-IV-V or ii-V-I, helping you to anticipate chord changes and create more effective bass lines.

Improvisation: The circle of fifths helps you understand which chords and scales work well together, making it easier to improvise and create melodic bass lines that fit harmonically within a song.

Transposing: Knowing the circle of fifths helps you to transpose songs into different keys when you perform with other musicians or adapt to vocal ranges.

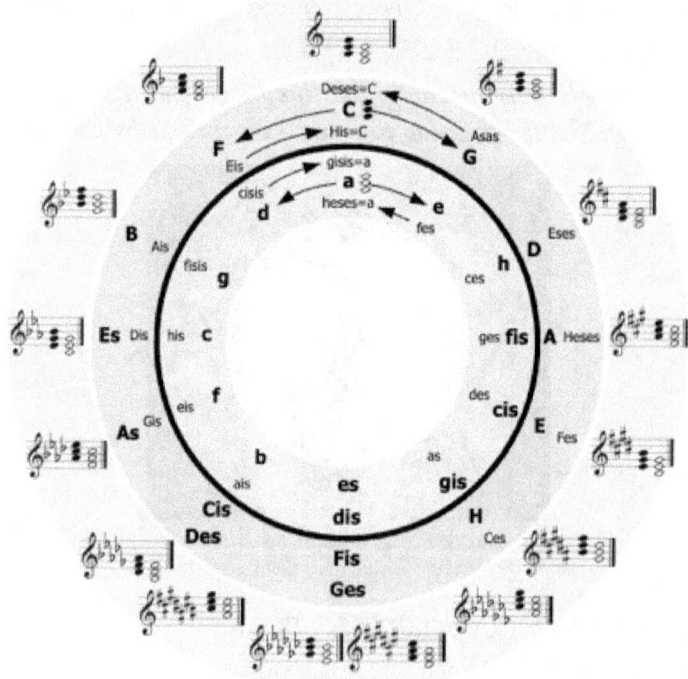

Circle of Fifths

SECTION TWO
LOCKING IN WITH THE DRUMMER

Locking in with the drummer forms the backbone of a band's rhythm section. A strong connection between the bassist and drummer creates a tight, cohesive groove that makes the music feel solid and engaging. A great bassist should also be able to help to keep an average drummer in time, holding back any rushing.

RHYTHMIC PARTNERSHIP

The bassist and drummer's relationship is about creating a unified rhythm and groove that supports the rest of the band. Each player complements the other, with the bassist often as the bridge between rhythm and harmony.

•**Kick Drum and Bass Lines:** One of the most fundamental aspects of locking in is aligning your bass notes with the drummer's kick drum. When your bass lines sync up with the kick drum, it reinforces the groove and gives the music a powerful, driving feel. Pay close attention to the drummer's patterns and adjust your bass lines to match or complement them.

•**Snare Drum and Rhythmic Accents:** While the kick drum provides the foundation, the snare often dictates where accents and syncopation occur. You can create a more dynamic feel by occasionally matching your bass notes with the snare or adding syncopated rhythms that interact with the snare's hits.

•**Hi-Hat and Cymbal Patterns:** The drummer's hi-hat and cymbal work add texture to the rhythm, and as a bassist, you can use these cues to add subtle rhythmic variations to your playing. For example, you might add ghost notes or muted plucks to match the hi-hat's "chick" sound, enhancing the groove's overall feel.

Understand how your bass lines interact with the kick, snare, and hi-hat patterns. Listen closely to the drummer's playing and adapt your rhythms to create a cohesive groove.

PRACTICING TO LOCK-IN YOUR TIMING

Regular practice with a drummer is crucial for developing a strong rhythmic connection. However, when a drummer isn't available, you can use a metronome or drum tracks to simulate that experience.

Practice with a Metronome: Set the metronome to different tempos and play simple bass lines, scales, or arpeggios along with it. Focus on locking in precisely with each click, treating the metronome as the drummer's kick drum.

Practice playing on the beat, behind the beat (slightly late), and ahead of the beat (slightly early). This will help you develop a feel for adapting your timing to different drumming styles and creating a more flexible groove.

Practice with Drum Tracks: Use drum loops or backing tracks that mimic actual drumming patterns. This allows you to practice matching your bass lines with kick, snare, and hi-hat patterns, making your playing more versatile and adaptable. Start with basic rock or funk grooves and gradually progress to more complex rhythms, such as jazz, Latin, or odd time signatures.

Key Point: Consistent practice with a metronome or drum tracks trains your ear and rhythm, helping you develop a sense of timing that will make it easier to lock in with a live drummer.

BUILDING YOUR GROOVE

You need to develop a strong sense of rhythm and timing to lock in with the drummer and create tight grooves. Here are some exercises to help:

"One-Note Groove" Exercise: Pick one note (e.g., E on the 7th fret of the A string) and play it in sync with the drummer's kick drum pattern or a metronome. Focus on hitting the note precisely with each beat or accent, ensuring you match the rhythm. Vary the rhythm by playing on different subdivisions (e.g., quarter notes, eighth notes, triplets, sixteenth notes) to improve your ability to adapt to different grooves.

"Call and Response" Exercise: With a drummer, practice a call-and-response exercise in which the drummer plays a simple rhythm or pattern, and you respond with a matching or complementary bass line, helping you to listen and respond in real-time, strengthening your rhythmic connection.

Ghost Notes and Muting: Practice adding ghost notes (muted plucks) between your main bass notes to mimic the rhythmic texture of the hi-hat or snare drum. Muted and ghost notes are subtle yet powerful techniques that bassists employ to enhance groove, rhythm, and expression within a bass line.

Muted notes are produced by lightly touching the strings with the fretting hand without pressing them down fully against the fretboard, effectively dampening the strings. When these muted strings are plucked with the picking hand, they produce a percussive, clicking sound rather than a pitched note, adding rhythmic complexity and stimulating drum patterns, making the bass line more dynamic and engaging.

On the other hand, **Ghost notes** are notes played very softly, almost imperceptible in volume, but still carry a muted pitch. They are executed by partially muting the string with the fretting hand while applying minimal plucking force. Ghost notes fill the spaces between the main notes, adding texture and subtle rhythmic nuances without overpowering the primary melody. By integrating muted and ghost notes, bassists create intricate patterns that contribute to the overall feel of the music, accentuate syncopation, and interact seamlessly with other rhythm section instruments to drive the groove forward.

Visualize Your Success – The more you practice these exercises, the more naturally you can create grooves that lock in tightly with the drummer's rhythms. In my early days, I would often find solace in prayer, seeking guidance and confidence before I stepped into my first gigs. It was all about visualizing my success. Fear, I realized, was just an impostor.

A dear friend **of mine, Frank Hamblen**, a 7-Time Championship-Winning NBA Coach with **Michael Jordan's** *Bulls* and **Kobe Bryant's** *Lakers*, motivated his players by saying:

"You just refuse to lose. True success is found in the relentless pursuit of excellence and the unwavering belief in your own potential."

NBA Coach Frank Hamblen and Tad Sisler
Source – Sisler Private Collection

So many people give up right when success is literally around the corner. Tell yourself, *"Failure is not an option."*

PLAYING IN THE POCKET

Playing "in the pocket" means being perfectly in sync with the drummer, creating a groove that feels effortless, steady, and rhythmically tight. It's about establishing a deep, locked-in connection that makes the music feel grounded and energetic.

Stay Relaxed: Playing in the pocket requires being relaxed and confident. Tension in your fingers, wrists, or shoulders can make your playing feel rushed or sloppy, so maintain a loose, comfortable posture.

Listen Actively: Listen to what the drummer is doing and adjust your playing accordingly. This might mean simplifying your bass line, adding rhythmic variations, or syncing more closely with the drummer's accents.

Consistency and Precision: Make sure every note you play is clear, consistent, and rhythmically precise. When you're in the pocket, each note should blend seamlessly with the drums, creating a groove that feels like one cohesive unit.

TIPS FOR DEVELOPING POCKET PLAYING

Practice simple bass lines that emphasize the downbeats, then gradually add syncopation and rhythmic variations as you become more comfortable. Record yourself playing with a drummer or drum track, then listen back to identify areas where your timing could be tighter.

Key Point: Playing in the pocket requires a deep understanding of rhythm, active listening, and the ability to adapt to the drummer's feel. This results in a groove that sounds tight and cohesive.

SECTION THREE
SYNCOPATION AND TIMING

Take all the elements I've just described and put them together, now focusing on developing syncopation and timing.

DEVELOPING A GROOVE

Emphasize off-beats or unexpected accents. Balance syncopation with space (playing in the pocket) to perfect the development of a natural groove. Practice with a metronome or drum track and listen to genres like funk and reggae for inspiration.

KEEPING TIME IN FAST PASSAGES

Set the metronome at a slow tempo, then increase the speed as you play. Stay relaxed to maintain your precision. Subdivide the beats into eighth notes, triplets, or sixteenth notes to improve the accuracy of your timing.

POLYRHYTHMS

Practice your basic 3 against 2 polyrhythms to develop independence and move on to more sophisticated polyrhythms. Listen and adapt to the drummer's patterns to sync with their rhythm. You can also influence the drummer to adjust to your patterns and nuances as you grow. Always lock into the main pulse, even when playing complex patterns.

ALWAYS PRIORITIZE YOUR POCKET PLAYING

Perfect the art of feeling the grove, staying in sync with the drummer. Concentrate on simplicity and rhythm over complexity until you are comfortable playing more sophisticated patterns. Always listen to adapt your playing and maintain a cohesive groove.

"When I was doing sessions, I played with three different drummers every day. You'd get to know the ones you'd have a nice time with and the ones who were going to be hard bloody work. As soon as I heard John Bonham play, I knew this was going to be great - somebody who knows what he's doing and swings like a bastard. We locked together as a team immediately." – John Paul Jones

John Paul Jones
Credit – Wikimedia Commons

Playing the bass requires technique. Performing requires the ability to adapt to audiences, different venues, and other musicians. Knowing the psychology of performance can help you become a completely rounded player.

CHAPTER FOUR
PSYCHOLOGICAL ASPECTS OF PERFORMING

No matter how much education I give you, or how much you learn from books, teachers, and mentors, experience is the real teacher. I became who I am through countless performances and recording sessions with the best players on the planet. You can accelerate your progress by getting as much experience as you possibly can, as quickly as you possibly can.

ARTIST SPOTLIGHT
STING

Sting
Credit – Flickr/Creativecommons.org

As a young adult in the 1980s, I saw amazing artists like **The Cars** and **David Bowie.** One of my favorite bands was **The Police**, led by **Gordon Matthew Thomas Sumner**, otherwise known as **Sting.** Their hits like *"Roxanne," "Every Breath You Take,"* and *"Message in a Bottle"* were groundbreaking. **Sting** had a hugely successful solo career, blending rock, jazz, reggae, and world music into his sophisticated recordings.

Believe it or not, **Sting** struggled with stage fright early in his career and even during his time leading **The Police.** He overcame it by shifting his mindset, viewing his performances as an opportunity to share his art rather than something to be judged. I had a similar mindset in my early career. I performed fine in front of large audiences, even in stadiums in front of a sea of people. Still, if I happened to see one great musician in the audience, I would immediately become intimidated, even trying to be perfect so they could only judge me positively. Like **Sting,** I learned to focus on the music and engage with the audience rather than fearing their reactions.

Although **Sting** plays guitar, keyboards, harmonica, and saxophone, he is most famous for his bass work, both in **The Police** and his solo work.

While you're focusing on syncopation, check out **Sting's** bass playing. He approaches the bass as a rhythmic and harmonic instrument, blending simple, driving root notes with more complex melodic lines. When you listen to **Sting,** you hear elements of reggae, jazz, and rock in his bass lines, but he does not overplay. **Sting** emphasizes the groove, leaving space to let other elements of the music shine. His use of syncopation and countermelodies should act as a clinic for your growth as a bassist. **Sting** is one of my favorites, and through his approach, he has become one of the most influential musicians in rock and pop history.

"I feel this music has nurtured me as I've been immersing myself in it. I've felt supported by it." – Sting

SECTION ONE
OVERCOMING STAGE FRIGHT

My dear friend, *Hall of Fame Major League Baseball* pitcher **Trevor Hoffman** held the record for the most saves in history for a time. When I interviewed him, I asked him about how he handled fear when he was on "the big stage." **Trevor** told me that his job was to instill fear in the batters who faced him. It was a psychological game that went above and beyond his ability or technique, although he had the most stellar change-up in baseball. **Trevor Hoffman** believed in positive visualization, in mentally preparing for a performance, and this approach worked miracles for him.

Tad Sisler with MLB Hall-of-Fame Pitcher Trevor Hoffman
Source – Sisler Private Collection

POSITIVE VISUALIZATION involves imagining yourself performing successfully on stage before the actual performance, reducing anxiety and building confidence.

Visualize Success: Spend a few minutes each day picturing yourself on stage, playing with ease, confidence, and enjoyment. Imagine the audience loving what you are playing and see yourself staying relaxed and in control.

Focus on the Details: Include as many details as possible in your visualization, such as the feel of your bass, the sound of the music, and the stage environment. This mental preparation helps create a sense of familiarity, making the actual performance feel less intimidating. Use visualization regularly, especially in the days before a performance, to build confidence and readiness.

PLAY YOUR ASS OFF

One of the most effective ways to overcome stage fright is to **become so proficient** on your instrument that you feel fully prepared and confident.

Practice Thoroughly: Invest time practicing your setlist until you can play it effortlessly, even under pressure. The more comfortable you are with your material, the less you'll worry about making mistakes on stage.

Simulate Performance Conditions: Practice performing in front of friends, family, or even a mirror to simulate the experience of being watched. This exercise helps reduce the fear of being on stage by making it a more familiar experience. The more prepared and proficient you are, the more confident you'll feel, reducing the likelihood of stage fright taking over.

BREATHING TECHNIQUES can be highly effective in calming nerves and reducing the physical symptoms of stage fright, such as rapid heart rate and shallow breathing.

Deep Breathing: Before going on stage, practice deep, slow breathing. Inhale deeply through your nose for a count of 4, hold for 4, and exhale slowly through your mouth for a count of 6-8.

This helps regulate your heart rate and relax your body.

Focus on Exhalation: Emphasize the exhale, as it activates the parasympathetic nervous system, which calms your body and reduces anxiety. If you feel nerves creeping in, use deep breathing not only before stepping on stage but also during the performance.

MINDFULNESS DURING PLAYING is about staying present and fully engaged in the moment. It helps reduce anxiety by keeping one's attention on the performance instead of worrying about potential mistakes or judgment.

Focus on the Music: Pay attention to the sound of your bass, the rhythm of the drums, and the overall groove. Let yourself get lost in the music rather than thinking about the audience or your nerves.

Use Your Senses: Tune into the sensations of playing—how your fingers feel on the strings, the vibrations of your instrument, and the sound of the notes. This will keep your mind anchored to the present moment. If you get nervous, gently bring your focus back to the music and the physical act of playing.

SECTION TWO
DEVELOPING STAGE PRESENCE

I've been a singer and a pianist/keyboardist for most of my career, so most of my performances onstage have been behind the piano or keyboards. Learning to stand up and sing without an instrument as a crutch was a stretch, and it took some time for me to feel comfortable doing it. A bassist can focus on his instrument and his ability as a player, which is a great starting point for learning stage presence. Learning to master the instrument is the first step. When you play with poise and confidence, the crowd immediately reacts positively.

CONFIDENCE, ENERGY AND POISE

Preparation is the foundation of confidence on stage. Practice your setlist until you can play it effortlessly. Doing this allows you to focus on engaging with the audience rather than worrying about making mistakes.

Positive Mindset: Approach each performance with a positive mindset. Performing on stage is an opportunity to share your music, not a test. Remember that the audience is there to enjoy the music. When you focus on people judging you, it hampers your ability to play with a positive mindset.

Start with Smaller Audiences: Build confidence by performing in front of smaller groups, starting with friends and family or at open mic nights. For me, it's actually easier to perform in front of large audiences than small groups.

I can get lost in performing in a stadium in front of a sea of people, but a group of eyes on me in an intimate setting can be intimidating. It helps if they appear welcoming and friendly, but either way, it is great practice.

Use Energy and Emotion: Let the energy and emotion of the music flow through you. Playing with enthusiasm and passion naturally makes you appear more confident, and the audience will respond to your energy. The more you enjoy playing, the more your confidence will shine through, creating a positive, infectious vibe for the audience.

BODY LANGUAGE

Maintain Eye Contact: Look out into the audience occasionally rather than staring at your instrument the entire time. If direct eye contact feels intimidating, look just above the heads of the crowd to create the illusion of eye contact.

Smile and Express Emotion: Smiling and showing facial expressions that match the song's mood help create a connection with the audience. It shows that you're enjoying the performance, encouraging them to enjoy it too.

Stand Tall with Good Posture: Stand up straight with your shoulders relaxed. Good posture exudes confidence and makes you look more engaged with the performance.

Avoid slouching or appearing closed off, as it can make you seem disinterested. Posture is also great for stamina if you are playing long gigs.

Move with the Music: Sway, nod your head or tap your foot in time with the rhythm. These small movements show you're actively feeling the music, making your performance appear more dynamic. Use open body language to appear approachable and engaged. Don't cross your arms or turn away from the audience, as it can create a barrier between you and them.

MOVING CONFIDENTLY ON STAGE

Start with Small Movements: Begin by incorporating subtle movements, like shifting your weight from one foot to the other or taking small steps while playing. Add more movement to your performance as you become more comfortable.

Interact with Band Members: Engage with your fellow musicians by moving towards them, exchanging smiles, or nodding in sync with their playing. This interaction makes the performance feel more cohesive and entertaining for the audience. Many of my bandmembers, especially guitarists, love to have that strange, insane look in their eyes as they play their solos, staring right at you like a lunatic! It's a rock and roll thing, I think, but it's kind of cool.

Practice Moving While Playing: Rehearse your set while moving around, maintaining your playing quality even when in motion. This practice helps you get used to navigating the stage and handling obstacles like cables or equipment.

Use the Stage Space: Take advantage of the entire stage by moving around during instrumental breaks or less demanding sections of your bass lines. Doing this creates a sense of movement and energy, making the performance more visually appealing. My granddaughter, *American Idol* Top 10 finalist **Makayla Phillips**, learned early to use the whole stage to captivate her audience. This is a great practice for a bass player when playing rehearsed music. It is a detriment, though, to move too far away from the drummer regularly. You want to always stay locked in as a cohesive rhythm section.

Always be mindful of your balance, with natural and fluid movements. Avoid making sudden, jerky motions that disrupt your playing or make you look uncomfortable. It's all about being smooth! Few of us are born stage performers. It's an acquired skill, but with helps to have the support of your family, friends, and fellow musicians. **Leland Sklar** is a great example:

ARTIST SPOTLIGHT
LELAND SKLAR
Leland Sklar is one of the most recorded and accomplished bassists in the previous half-century.

His bass is on a string of hits going back as far as the 1970s, with a group of studio musicians including **Russ Kunkel, Steve Postell, Danny Kortchmar,** and **Waddy Wachtel**. All these players were comfortable in the studio. Still, they toured with the headliners they recorded, including **James Taylor, Linda Ronstadt, Don Henley,** and **Carole King.**

Although they were more comfortable in the studio, they became excellent stage musicians, later forming their own group, **Immediate Family.** Study **Leland Sklar's** effortless performance on complicated bass lines and techniques as applied to his recorded songs. He was an innovator who created iconic bass lines that were as instrumental in making song hits as were the lyrics and music.

Leland Sklar
Credit – Wikimedia Commons

"My whole family was very supportive of my choice in a career. I started playing music when I was about six years old." – Leland Sklar

SECTION THREE
PLAYING IN HIGH-PRESSURE SITUATIONS

When you get to the point where you find yourself auditioning, doing a live recording session, or playing in front of a large crowd, use these strategies to succeed:

PREPARING FOR AN AUDITION

Know Your Material: Thoroughly learn the audition pieces and any potential songs that may be requested. Be ready to play them in various keys, tempos, and styles, which shows versatility and adaptability.

Practice Sight-Reading: Many auditions involve sight-reading, so practice reading sheet music, chord charts, and tablature regularly to improve your skills. Being a confident sight-reader can set you apart from other bassists.

Warm Up Before the Audition: Arrive early at the audition location and warm up your hands and fingers. This helps prevent nerves from affecting your playing and ensures you're ready to perform at your best. **Tune your bass!**

DURING THE AUDITION

Stay Relaxed and Confident: Take a few deep breaths before you begin playing to calm your nerves. Remember that you're there to showcase your skills, not prove yourself perfect.

Listen and Adapt: If you're auditioning with other musicians, listen carefully to them and adapt your playing to fit the group. Demonstrating your ability to lock in with others is a valuable trait for a bassist.

Display Your Range: If given the opportunity, showcase different techniques (fingerstyle, slap, pick playing) and musical styles to demonstrate your versatility. Confidence comes from preparation. The more you've practiced and anticipated potential challenges, the more likely you will perform well in an audition.

PREPARING FOR STUDIO SESSIONS

Know the Material Inside Out: Before entering the studio, familiarize yourself with the songs and arrangements.

Practice along with a metronome to ensure you're playing in perfect time, as recording sessions demand precision.

Bring the Right Gear: Make sure your bass is well-maintained, with fresh strings and in-tune. Bring any necessary equipment, such as pedals, picks, or spare cables, to avoid unnecessary interruptions during the session.

Stay Flexible: Be prepared for changes or adjustments. Sometimes, producers or other musicians might request alterations to a song's bass line or feel, so be adaptable and ready to adjust on the fly.

DURING THE RECORDING SESSION

Focus on Consistency: Recording sessions can be long, and you may need to play the same part multiple times. Maintain consistent timing, dynamics, and tone across takes.

Don't Overthink Mistakes: If you make a mistake, stay calm and keep going. Fixing errors or punching in a specific section is often easier than restarting the entire take. Treat the recording session as an opportunity to capture your best performance rather than a high-pressure test. This mindset shift helps you stay relaxed and focused. Back when I started working in tape-based recording environments, we paid for each minute of recording time, and if we made a mistake, we could mess up the whole take, so it was unnerving. Today, it is so much easier to use computer-based recording. Mistakes can be edited or removed without losing the take. So, relax and know you can get your best performance without worrying about each take.

PERFORMING IN FRONT OF LARGE CROWDS

Practice Performance Skills: Rehearse your setlist in a way that mimics the live performance environment, incorporating stage movements and audience engagement. If possible, practice under different lighting or sound conditions.

Know Your Parts Cold: Ensure that you know your bass lines inside and out so you're not thinking about the notes while performing. This allows you to focus on connecting with the audience and enjoying the experience.

DURING THE PERFORMANCE

Stay Present: Focus on the music, your bandmates, and the crowd's energy. Don't get overwhelmed by the number of people or the scale of the venue. Treat it as an extension of your rehearsals.

Feed off the Crowd's Energy: Use the crowd's energy and enthusiasm to fuel your performance. Smile, move with the music, and engage with the audience to create a more enjoyable experience for both you and them. Remember that the audience is there to enjoy the music. They want you to succeed, so embrace the moment and have fun.

The best way to succeed as quickly as possible is to get into a routine where you practice as much as you can. Practice makes perfect. It's an old saying but it still rings true.

CHAPTER FIVE
STRUCTURING AN EFFECTIVE PRACTICE ROUTINE

A recent government study revealed that many musicians don't maximize their practice time, especially when they become more experienced. As they become more proficient, work increases, and family responsibility cut in to their practice time. In the same study, we learned that the most helpful practice strategies were listening to recordings, slow practice, and maintaining a mindset of self-awareness and focus. Simply picking up their instrument helped them to stay motivated. Taking breaks was also helpful. Source-Eric.ed.gov

SECTION ONE
SETTING ACHIEVABLE GOALS

SHORT-TERM GOALS

Focus on Specific Skills: Set daily or weekly goals targeting specific techniques or areas, like learning a new scale, improving finger dexterity, or mastering a particular song. This will keep your practice sessions focused and productive.

Keep Goals Attainable: Aim for goals that challenge you but are realistic within a short timeframe. For example, practice a challenging bass riff for 15 minutes daily or aim to master a new groove by the end of the week.

Breaking down larger goals into smaller, manageable tasks helps prevent overwhelm and allows you to see steady progress.

"I'm a big believer of daylight in the studio." — Geddy Lee

Geddy Lee
Credit — Wikimedia Commons

LONG-TERM GOALS
Set Clear Milestones: Identify significant goals, like preparing for a concert, audition, or recording project. Break these down into monthly or quarterly objectives, such as learning all the songs in your setlist or improving your slap bass technique.

Develop a Timeline: Create a schedule leading up to the event, assigning specific tasks or skills to different weeks or months. Doing this gets you prepared and allows for consistent progress toward your larger goal. Adjust your long-term goals based on your progress to stay on track without feeling pressured.

TRACK YOUR PROGRESS
Record Achievements and Challenges: Use a practice journal to document what you practice each day, noting any improvements, difficulties, or techniques you focus on. Keeping a journal helps identify patterns in your learning and areas that need more attention.

Reflect Regularly: Review your journal weekly or monthly to assess your progress, celebrate achievements, and adjust your goals as needed. Tracking progress motivates and holds you accountable, making it easier to stay committed to your practice routine.

MAKE A DIFFERENCE WITH YOUR BOOK REVIEW
Unlock the Power of Generosity

"Helping others is the true reward."

I've been playing music for nearly fifty years, working with some of the best bass players around. I've learned the instrument forwards and backwards to get a greater understanding of the critical role a bass commands in bands, ensembles, and recordings. Learning to play bass is about more than just hitting the right notes; it's about timing, groove, and being the heartbeat of the band.

Would you help someone just like you—curious about playing bass but unsure where to start, or already a great player but always wanting to refine and improve?

My mission is to make bass playing easy, rewarding, and fun for everyone.

But to reach more people, I need your help.

Most people choose books based on reviews. So, I'm asking you to help another bass player by leaving a review.

It doesn't cost anything and takes less than a minute, but it could change someone's musical journey. Your review could help...

- ...one more person find their rhythm.
- ...one more student feel confident in learning.
- ...one more musician bring life to the beat.
- ...one more dream come true.

If you purchased my book on Amazon, here's the link to leave your review:

https://www.amazon.com/review/review-your-purchases/?asin=1966258046

Or, you can just scan this QR code to get to the Amazon review page:

If you love helping others, you're my kind of person. Thank you from the bottom of my heart!

Tad Sisler

My friend, former star *NBA* basketball player and businessman **Earvin "Magic" Johnson** has been known for keeping himself accountable, demanding excellence, and always planning for the future. **Magic** said:

"I look three to five years ahead, not ten years behind."

Tad Sisler on the Lakers Bench with Magic Johnson
Source – Sisler Private Collection

SECTION TWO
DAILY PRACTICE ROUTINES

Keep a well-structured daily practice routine and you'll stay ahead of the game in progress.

WARM-UP EXERCISES

Hand Stretches: Begin each session with finger and wrist stretches to prevent injury and loosen up your muscles. Stretches are especially important for bass players, because your instrument's thicker strings and larger fretboard require more hand strength. Developing callouses on your hands and fingers will happen, and most bass players will tell you it helps to have callouses, especially while playing through long gigs or recording sessions. It's your body's protective mechanism against broken skin.

Scales and Arpeggios: Practice basic scales (e.g., major, minor, chromatic) and arpeggios to warm up your fingers and improve muscle memory. Start slow, focusing on accuracy and even tone. Like developing callouses, warming up also prepares your hands for more demanding practice and reduces the risk of strain.

TIME MANAGEMENT: Breaking up practice sessions into focused segments helps you to balance your development across different areas of playing. Here's a suggestion:

Technique (15-20 minutes): Focus on fingerstyle, slap bass, or string skipping techniques. Incorporate exercises like chromatic scales or "spider" drills to build dexterity.

Rhythm (15 minutes): Work on rhythm exercises, including syncopation, ghost notes, and playing with a metronome or drum track to improve timing.

Repertoire (20-30 minutes): Practice songs you're working on, paying attention to difficult sections. Break them into smaller parts and repeat them slowly before gradually increasing the tempo.

"You have to get up and plant the seed and see if it grows, but you can't just wait around, you have to water it and take care of it."
- Bootsy Collins

William "Bootsy" Collins
Credit — Wikimedia Commons

METRONOME PRACTICE

Again, timing is the most important skill you can develop to play in a groove with a band or while recording. Using a metronome (or click track, or drum program locked to a tempo) helps you to learn how to stay locked into the rhythm.

Start Slow: Practice scales, arpeggios, or grooves using a metronome. Begin at a slow tempo (60-80 BPM) to focus on accuracy, then gradually increase the speed as you become more comfortable.

Subdivision Practice: To build rhythmic versatility, work on playing quarter notes, eighth notes, triplets, and sixteenth notes at the same tempo.

Consistency: Regular metronome practice improves timing, making your playing tighter and more reliable, especially when playing with other musicians.

SECTION THREE
AVOIDING BURNOUT

Burnout can occur for many reasons. In my experience, the only times I ever felt burnout were when I didn't take care of myself physically and mentally. The music, the gigs, recording and editing, and taking care of my family were all joys to me. Legendary **Metallica** bassist **Cliff Burton** had an interesting take on burnout. He said:

"You don't burn out from going too fast. You burn out from going too slow and getting bored."

Here are some ideas on how you can avoid burnout:

MIXING UP PRACTICE TO STAY ENGAGED

Rotate Between Different Skills: To keep practice sessions fresh, go back and forth between different aspects of bass playing, like fingerstyle technique, slap bass, scales, rhythm work, and improvisation. This will help to prevent monotony while you are developing multiple skills simultaneously.

Incorporate New Styles: Experimenting with different genres (funk, jazz, rock, reggae, etc.) can introduce new challenges and keep things exciting. Learning different rhythms and grooves can help break up the routine and stimulate creativity.

Playing Along with Songs: Playing with your favorite tracks or new genres adds fun to your practice while reinforcing practical applications of your technical skills. Mixing up exercises and styles keeps your practice fresh, prevents boredom, and challenges you in new ways.

RECOGNIZE WHEN TO TAKE BREAKS

Schedule Regular Breaks: Taking short breaks during practice sessions (every 20-30 minutes) allows your brain and fingers to rest. These breaks can prevent mental fatigue and help maintain focus throughout the practice session.

Watch for Physical Strain: Playing the bass, with its thicker strings and larger fretboard, can put physical stress on your fingers, wrists, and back. If you feel discomfort, stopping and stretching or taking a more extended break is important to prevent injury.

Mental Reset: If you feel mentally drained or uninspired, take a day off from playing to engage in other creative activities like listening to music, reading, or meditating. If I need to get away from it for a minute, returning later with a fresh outlook helps reset my mind and allows me to come back strong. Also, regular breaks help prevent physical strain and keep my mind sharp and motivated for continued learning.

REWARD YOURSELF FOR PROGRESS

Set Achievable Goals: Breaking down significant goals into smaller milestones (e.g., mastering a song, learning a new scale, or improving a technique) helps keep you motivated and gives you a clear sense of progress.

Celebrate Small Wins: When you reach a big or small goal, take time to acknowledge your achievement. Reward yourself by playing a song you love, buying new gear, or taking a day off to enjoy your progress.

Stay Positive: Focus on what you've accomplished rather than what you still need to do. Celebrating progress builds confidence and helps you maintain a positive mindset, reducing the likelihood of burnout.

Another great way to avoid burnout and stay fresh is to explore and master as many different types of music as you can.

CHAPTER SIX
MASTERING MULTIPLE GENRES OF MUSIC

As a kid, many different musicians and bands influenced my style. My father loved show tunes, my mother was a classical pianist, my sisters were into rock and roll, and as I grew, I learned to embrace multiple genres. My grandfather had a saying, ***"The house of music has many rooms, including the outhouse!"*** You may not like everything you hear, but the more you listen to and learn to appreciate diverse music, the faster you grow. I remember seeing one rock band, just three musicians led by **Eric Clapton,** playing in huge stadiums all over the world, and I wondered how just three guys could make so much music together. The group was **Cream,** with **Ginger Baker** on drums and **Jack Bruce** on bass. **Jack Bruce** was a rare performer who embraced multiple genres, from classical to jazz to blues to rock.

ARTIST SPOTLIGHT
JACK BRUCE

Jack Bruce
Credit – Wikimedia Commons

Born in Scotland in 1943, **Jack Bruce's** work with **Cream** in the late 1960s brought him international fame, contributing his virtuosic bass playing and as a vocalist and songwriter, co-writing classics like *"Sunshine of Your Love"* and *"White Room."* Beyond **Cream, Bruce** played with the **Graham Bond Organisation, John Mayall & the Bluesbreakers**, and **West, Bruce & Laing.**

Jack Bruce's bass playing style was a revolutionary blend of melody, rhythm, and improvisation. Unlike many bassists of his era who stuck to traditional supportive roles, Bruce approached the bass as a harmonic and melodic instrument, often playing counter-melodies or improvising alongside the lead guitar. This style was one of the elements that made **Cream** work with only three players. He filled the holes with his intricate style. **Bruce's** jazz background gave him a deep understanding of chord progressions and modal playing, allowing him to write and play intricate bass lines that transcended typical rock and blues structures. He was known for using the *Gibson EB-3* bass, which helped him achieve his signature warm, growling tone that became a hallmark of his sound.

Technically, **Bruce** employed a mixture of fingerpicking and plucking, often using a more aggressive attack on the strings to produce a rich, full sound. His ability to blend intricate, jazz-inspired runs with bluesy, hard-hitting rock lines made him a unique figure in bass playing. **Bruce** was also an accomplished singer, often performing lead vocals while maintaining complex bass lines, adding a distinctive layer to his performances. His improvisational skills, particularly in live settings, helped redefine what a bassist could achieve within a rock band, influencing generations of musicians who followed.

"What I used to play was rhythm guitar before I saw Jack Bruce. I said, that's what I want to do in life. He was definitely the main influence." — *Geezer Butler*

SECTION ONE
JAZZ BASS TECHNIQUES

One of my favorite modern bassists is **Esperanza Spalding**. In her vocal and bass performances and compositions, she blends genres, combining jazz, R&B, Funk, and classical elements. **Spalding** won the *Grammy Award* for *Best New Artist* in 2011, helping her to gain international acclaim.

Esperanza Spalding
Credit – Wikimedia Commons

As noted in Esperanza Spalding's performances, great jazz bass playing requires a blend of harmony, rhythm, and improvisation, whether you're playing an upright or bass guitar.

WALKING BASSLINES are the hallmark of jazz bass, especially in swing and bebop styles. You provide the harmonic and rhythmic foundation, playing a continuous sequence of quarter notes and "walking" through the chord changes.

Outlining Chord Progressions: A walking bass line usually centers around the root, third, fifth, and seventh notes of each chord, reinforcing the harmonic structure while maintaining a steady rhythm.

Approach Notes: To help a walking bassline breathe, a player will use approach notes (chromatic or diatonic) to lead into the next chord tone, adding a sense of motion and flow and connecting the chords smoothly.

Syncopation and Variations: To keep the walking bassline interesting, vary your rhythms, occasionally syncopating or adding triplets and rests, depending on the style of jazz you are playing. Remember always not to get "too busy." Keep your playing nuanced and tasteful.

Example: Playing a 2-5-1 progression (Dmin7–G7–Cmaj7) in a walking bassline, you might play D, F, A, C for the Dmin7 chord, G, B, D, F for the G7 chord, and C, E, G, B for the Cmaj7 chord, with chromatic approach notes leading into each new chord.

Example Music: Study **Paul Chambers** walking bass line on *"So What"*, by **Miles Davis**. Listen to the precision and energy of **Oscar Pettiford's** bass work on *"A Night In Tunisia"* by **Charlie Parker**. **Jymie Merritt's** bass line provides a deep groove in *"Moanin"*, by **Art Blakey & The Jazz Messengers**. Check out the innovative and melodic bass line of **Scott LaFaro** on the track *"Autumn Leaves"*, by the **Bill Evans Trio**. **Charlie Mingus** plays a soulful and emotional bass line in *"Goodbye Pork Pie Hat"*, his tribute to **Lester Young**.

BASIC IMPROVISATION

Jazz emphasizes **improvisation**, and you can play a critical role in this dynamic by supporting harmonic shifts and creating melodic lines.

Chord Tones and Scales: During improvisation, you can focus on chord tones (root, third, fifth, and seventh) to stay connected to the harmonic structure. Know your scales and arpeggios for each chord. For instance, becoming familiar with jazz scales, like the Dorian, Mixolydian, and Locrian modes, helps you create melodic improvisations. These scales allow you to move freely over different chords while maintaining the right mood.

Rhythmic Variations: Experiment with syncopation, triplets, or rests during solos to add rhythmic creativity.

Call and Response: In many jazz settings, improvisation involves a "call and response" between the bassist and other musicians, especially the drummer, allowing for a more interactive and spontaneous performance. Be prepared when trading 4's or 8's to play a sophisticated solo.

USING SCALES AND MODES IN IMPROVISATION

Scales and Modes as Foundations: Understanding and utilizing scales (major, minor, pentatonic, and blues scales) and modes (like Dorian, Mixolydian, and Aeolian) provide the melodic and harmonic framework for improvisation.

Application: By applying appropriate scales and modes over chord progressions, bassists can craft bass lines that complement the music harmonically. *Example*: The Dorian mode can add a jazzy feel over a minor chord progression.

PRACTICE TIPS

Learn Scales in All Positions: Practice scales across the entire fretboard to gain flexibility.

Interval Recognition: Understand the intervals within scales to navigate them more musically.

Improvise Over Backing Tracks: Use recordings to practice applying scales and modes in real time.

DEVELOPING YOUR UNIQUE STYLE

Explore Various Genres: Delve into different musical styles to absorb a wide range of influences.

Listen and Learn: Study the playing styles of diverse bassists to identify elements you can incorporate into your playing.

EXPERIMENTATION

Rhythmic Variation: Play with different rhythms and time signatures.

Articulation Techniques: Use slides, bends, harmonics, and muting to add character.

SELF-EXPRESSION

Emotional Connection: Let your feelings guide your improvisation to make it more authentic.

Storytelling: Think of your solo as telling a story with a beginning, development, and conclusion.

FEEDBACK AND REFLECTION

Record Yourself: Listening back can reveal areas for improvement and ideas for new approaches.

Seek Constructive Critique: Collaborate with others to gain new perspectives.

CRAFTING COMPELLING SOLOING TECHNIQUES

MELODIC DEVELOPMENT

Motifs and Themes: Create and develop simple melodic ideas throughout your solo.

Phrasing: Use rests and note lengths thoughtfully to shape musical sentences.

HARMONIC AWARENESS

Chord Tone Emphasis: Focus on chord tones (root, third, fifth, seventh) to ensure your solo aligns harmonically.

Tension and Release: Incorporate non-chord tones to build tension, resolving them to chord tones.

RHYTHMIC CREATIVITY

Syncopation: Use off-beat rhythms to add interest.

Polyrhythms: Introduce complex rhythms for advanced expression.

TECHNICAL SKILLS

Dynamic Control: Vary your volume to add emotional depth.

Articulation: Utilize techniques like staccato, legato, and vibrato for expressiveness.

INTERACTION WITH THE BAND

Listen to what other musicians are playing. Respond accordingly.

Space: Allow moments of silence within your solo for musical breathing room.

BOWING AND PLUCKING ON UPRIGHT

While most jazz bass playing is done **pizzicato** (plucking the strings), some jazz bassists incorporate **arco** (bowing) techniques for solo sections or specific pieces.

Pizzicato: When plucking, use the side of the index finger to pull the string, producing a warm, resonant tone. Jazz pizzicato involves a more rhythmic, percussive approach, usually in sync with the swing feel of the music.

Arco (Bowing): Bowing can be used in jazz to create sustained, lyrical passages, especially in ballads or when the bassist takes a solo. The key to successful arco playing in jazz is to control the bow pressure and angle to maintain smooth, expressive phrasing. Bowing is also visually appealing to the audience, showing your versatility.

Finger Independence: On the upright bass, you can use a 1-2-4 finger system (index, middle, pinky), which is great for playing fast passages or smoothly shifting between octaves.

JAZZ FUSION

Fusion blends jazz with other genres like rock, funk, and electronic music, requiring a different approach to bass playing.

Electric Bass in Fusion: In jazz fusion, the electric bass can take on a more melodic role, using slap bass, popping techniques, and chordal playing to add texture and complexity.

Rhythmic Complexity: Fusion typically involves complex time signatures and syncopation, so be comfortable playing in odd meters (e.g., 7/8 or 5/4) while maintaining the groove.

Extended Harmonies: Fusion bassists often play extended chord tones (e.g., ninths, elevenths, and thirteenths) or incorporate modal improvisation to complement the extended harmonies used in fusion compositions.

Example Music: Check out **Jaco Pastorius'** fretless bass on *"Birdland"* by **Weather Report.** Study the virtuostic technique blended with deep groove on **Stanley Clarke's** bass on the track *"Spain"*, by **Chick Corea.** Marcus Miller's groove on electric bass, but with upright techniques, on *"Tutu"*, by **Miles Davis,** defines this track. Listen to **Rick Laird** anchoring the complex rhythms and time signatures of *"The Inner Mounting Flame"*, by **Mahavishnu Orchestra.**

LEARN SUBTLE NUANCES BETWEEN NOTES

In jazz, the **subtle nuances** between notes—such as **ghost notes**, slides, and **muting**—are critical to creating a smooth, organic feel.

Ghost Notes: Play lightly muted or ghost notes percussively without a defined pitch, adding rhythmic complexity and groove. Ghost Notes are often used in faster swing or funk-influenced jazz.

Sliding: Sliding into notes creates a fluid, legato sound. For example, sliding from a half step below into a chord tone in walking basslines adds a bluesy or expressive touch.

Muted Plucks: Use your fretting hand to lightly touch the string while plucking, producing a muted sound that adds rhythmic texture to bass lines.

The most effective way to improve quickly is to listen to and learn from the experts. **Tony Robbins**, a great motivator, uses this approach in his seminars. My old friend, **President Gerald R. Ford,** knew this concept well when he said:

"I had a lot of experience with people smarter than I am."

President Gerald R. Ford and Tad Sisler
Source – Sisler Private Collection

SECTION TWO:
ROCK AND POP BASS

There's a powerful feeling when driving a band with your bass, locking into the drum beat and laying down the foundation upon which all the other musicians can shine. Here are some techniques for mastering rock and pop bass:

SYNCOPATED POP GROOVES

Emphasizing Off-Beats: In pop music, you can create catchy grooves by emphasizing off-beats, using syncopation to add bounce and movement. Instead of only playing on the downbeats (1, 2, 3, 4), syncopated grooves emphasize the "and" of each beat, adding a dynamic rhythm that drives the song forward.

Pop Bass Grooves: Pop basslines can follow chord progressions tightly, but syncopation makes them stand out. Techniques like playing ghost notes, as described in our jazz bass section, or adding small embellishments between beats keep the groove engaging without overcomplicating.

Example Music: Classic pop songs like **Michael Jackson's** *"Billie Jean"* feature minimal but highly effective syncopated basslines with carefully placed notes between beats. Classic, unforgettable bass lines like the bass part on the **Temptations'** *"My Girl"* are a part of our fabric, and sometimes, they stand out more than any other part of the track. Practice with a metronome or drum track, focusing on playing on and between beats to master syncopation.

ROCK POWER CHORDS

Root and Fifth Power Chords: In rock music, you can emphasize **power chords**, the root and the fifth note of the chord. This adds a powerful, driving sound without clashing with the guitar.

Adding Punch: To create a more aggressive and punchy sound, try palm muting (lightly muting the strings with the side of the hand) or picking aggressively. Using a pick for harder attacks and more clarity in faster rock songs can give the bass line a sharp, defined sound.

Overdrive/Distortion: Many rock bassists use overdrive or distortion pedals to add grit and weight to their sound, helping the bass stand out in heavily amplified environments. Practice playing with power and consistency to make your bass lines sound bigger while ensuring they complement the distorted guitars.

Example Music: **John Entwistle** uses power chords during his bass solo in *"My Generation"*, by **The Who.** In *"The Lemon Song"* by **Led Zeppelin, John Paul Jones** delivers a dynamic bass performance mixing bluesy riffs with power chords.

One of my favorite rock bassists is **Tal Wilkenfeld**. Even as a young prodigy, she blended rock, jazz, and funk into her style, performing and touring with

Jeff Beck, Herbie Hancock, and **Prince. Tal Wilkenfeld** is a powerhouse. She is a great example of foundational playing, locking-in with drums and bass.

Tal Wilkenfeld
Credit – Wikimedia Commons

COMPLEMENTING GUITAR RHYTHMS

Locking in with Guitar Riffs: You can support the guitar by playing basslines that follow the basic chord progression while adding rhythmic or melodic variations. Be mindful of where the guitarist accents rhythms or chords and complement them by emphasizing the root notes or filling in gaps.

Creating Contrast: In some cases, playing simpler, steady basslines while the guitarist plays more complex riffs can create balance in the arrangement. Or, you could add movement when the guitar plays open chords by playing syncopated or rhythmically diverse lines. Remember, playing in a band or on a recording is about space and interplay. Always leave room for others to shine; give it your all when it's your turn.

Interplay with Drums: You should also align with the drummer's kick drum while supporting the guitar, creating a solid foundation for the band while giving your bass room to groove with the guitar. Listen closely to how the guitarist plays, and aim to reinforce or contrast their rhythms, depending on the song's dynamic needs.

BE THE DRIVING FORCE

Rhythm Section Backbone: In rock and pop, the bass is part of the rhythm section, locking in with the drums to form the backbone of the band's sound. A solid bassline can give the entire band a sense of direction and energy, particularly during transitions or building up to a chorus.

Creating Momentum: Bassists often create forward momentum in a song. In high-energy rock tracks, for instance, you can push the groove by playing slightly ahead of the beat, creating urgency. In contrast, pulling slightly behind the beat in ballads or slower pop songs can add a laid-back feel.

Dynamic Control: The bass plays an important role in controlling the dynamics of a performance. In quieter sections, you may want to play simpler, softer lines to let other instruments shine, while in choruses or climaxes, the bass might become louder, more aggressive, or more rhythmically complex. Be aware of the song's overall structure, using your bass playing to control the energy levels and keep the song moving forward.

SECTION THREE
CLASSICAL AND ORCHESTRAL BASS

Performing in classical and orchestral settings is usually structured. Being the foundational sound of a large ensemble is a powerful feeling, and it completes the overall sound in many ways.

BOWING TECHNIQUES
Producing Clean, Powerful Sound: Classical bassists typically use **arco** (bowing) to create a rich, resonant tone. As I mentioned in another chapter, two primary bow grips are used: the **French bow** (overhand) and the **German bow** (underhand). Producing a clean, powerful sound involves controlling the **bow pressure**, speed, and placement on the string (closer to the bridge for more power, further away for a softer tone). Consistent, smooth bowing is essential for maintaining tonal quality and volume.

UNDERSTANDING ORCHESTRAL SCORES
Reading Orchestral Music: Bassists need to follow the **bass clef** in orchestral scores and be adept at reading various time signatures, dynamics, and articulations. Orchestral parts often contain long rests, so it's really important to count accurately and be attentive to **cues from the conductor** or other sections of the orchestra. Bassists must also be familiar with **transposing instruments** and understand how their part fits into the overall orchestral arrangement. Refer to our section on books and online resources for a complete tutorial on reading scores and basic orchestral performance.

BLENDING WITH ENSEMBLES

Playing in Harmony: In both orchestras and chamber groups, the double bass is responsible for providing the harmonic foundation. You must focus on **intonation** and blending your sound with the cellos and other lower-register instruments. Dynamics are not just important; it's necessary to adjust your volume and tone to match the ensemble, making sure your bass supports rather than overpowers the other sections. Adaptability is a key skill for any bassist.

Example Music: The bass section plays a pivotal role in driving the drama and intensity of **Beehoven's** *"Symphony No. 5"*, particularly in the final movement. The contrabass parts in **Igor Stavinsky's** *"The Rite of Spring"* add to the dissonant, primal energy, particularly during *"Dance of the Earth."* The contrabass provides a deep, resonant foundation in *"Pines of Rome"* by **Ottorino Respighi**, enhancing the grandeur of this symphonic tone poem, especially in *"Pines of the Appian Way."*

SECTION FOUR
MASTERING OTHER GENRES

To master bass playing across different genres, you need to work on profoundly understanding each genre's rhythm, tone, and role in the music. Focus on syncing with the rhythm section (drums/percussion) for groove-heavy styles like funk, reggae, and Latin.

Explore tonal qualities (rounder tones in reggae and country, sharper, slap tones in funk).

Learn genre-specific techniques like slap bass, walking basslines, and syncopation. Here's how to approach some of the most influential genres:

REGGAE: Study and emulate the "one-drop" rhythm, placing the emphasis on the third beat of a four-beat measure. Work on locking in with the drum's kick on the off-beats to create a laid-back, deep groove. Play closer to the neck or use flat-wound strings to create a muted, round tone. Minimalism is important; reggae bass lines are simple but groove-driven.

Example Music: Listen to **Aston "Family Man" Barrett** of **The Wailers** on *"Stir it Up"* and other tracks for deep, rhythmic basslines that carry the weight of the groove. **Robbie Shakespeare** plays deep, rolling bass lines on a number of tracks by **Peter Tosh**, including *"Legalize it"*, and *"Get up, Stand Up."*

WORLD MUSIC bass playing can vary greatly depending on the region. The best way to emulate the specific genre is to study approaches by prominent bass players in that region. For African-inspired music, bassists often play polyrhythmic patterns mirroring traditional percussion instruments. In Indian music, bassists sometimes emulate the drone sound by using sustained notes. Be flexible with your tone. You can mimic traditional instruments and rhythms using different effects and techniques (thumb picking or slapping).

Example: Victor Wooten often incorporates world music influences into his playing, blending complex rhythms and scales with modern bass techniques. Learning the nuances of new genres will absolutely influence your playing across the board.

> *"What I'm trying to do, in my own small way, is trying to bring African and Afro-Cuban rhythms into rock." — Jack Bruce*

LATIN MUSIC features rhythms incorporating the clave or tumbao, and the bass often plays a prominent role in driving these grooves. Lock in with the percussion, providing a steady, syncopated groove that complements the off-beat accents of the congas and timbales. A punchy, percussive tone is often preferred. Playing with your fingers or using palm muting can help achieve this effect.

Example Music: Listen to the work of **Cachao**, especially on his tracks *"Cachao's Guajira Ritmo"* and *"Descargas" (Cuban Jam sessions)*. **Cachao** is a master of the Latin bass style, primarily in mambo and salsa. The bass line in **Santana's** *"Oye Como Va"* by **David Brown** is a driving force, but I personally like **Tito Puente's** version better. I had the pleasure of opening for **Tito Puente** years ago, and I was literally overwhelmed by the intensity and perfection of his twenty-five-piece acoustic band. **Orlando "Cachaíto" López** plays a warm, steady pulse in *"Chan Chan"*, by **Buena Vista Social Club,** complementing the traditional Cuban rhythms and giving the track its soulful, nostalgic fee.

FUNK bass is all about syncopation and groove, strongly emphasizing slap and pop techniques. Funk basslines are typically tight and rhythmic and focus on the drum interaction to create a driving beat. A bright, cutting tone helps the bass stand out in the mix, mainly when using slap techniques.

James Jamerson was the 'godfather of funk' (check out the entire *"What's Going On"* album by **Marvin Gaye**. Jamerson said:

"My feel was always an Eastern feel. A spiritual thing. Take 'Standing in the Shadows of Love'...the bass line has an Arabic feel. I've been around a whole lot of people from the East, from China and Japan. Then I studied the African, Cuban and Indian scales. I brought all that with me to Motown."

Example Music: Bootsy Collins (check out his bass on *"Flash Light"* by **Parliament**, or his solo work including *"Give Up the Funk (Tear the Roof off the Sucker)"*, and *"Bootzilla"*) and **Larry Graham** are pioneers of the slap technique in funk and are known for their high-energy, rhythmic playing. **Graham's** slap bass technique revolutionized funk bass playing, as evidenced in *"Thank you (Falettinme Be Mice Elf Agin)"* by **Sly & the Family Stone**. The essence of funk bass playing was gleaned from many different genres.

COUNTRY

The "walking bassline" is commonly used in country music, where the bassist plays steady quarter or half notes that outline the chord changes. In more modern country music, you may find more syncopation and groove. Most country bassists achieve a warm, round tone by playing with the fingers or using a pick for a more percussive sound.

Example Music: Country bassists like **Michael Rhodes** blend traditional walking basslines with modern elements to keep the rhythm section solid yet melodic. **Mike Chapman** plays a supportive, laid-back vibe on *"Friends in Low Places"*, by **Garth Brooks**. Check out the simple yet driving bass line by **Marshall Grant** on *"Folsom Prison Blues"* by **Johnny Cash**.

BLUES basslines often use 12-bar progressions and are heavily influenced by pentatonic scales. Lock into the groove while supporting the soloists. Aim for a warm, rounded tone while supporting the groove and rhythm.

Example Music: Willie Dixon's walking bass on *"Hoochie Coochie Man"* by **Muddy** Waters is perfect. **Donald "Duck" Dunn** provided the rhythmic backbone for many classic *Stax Records* hits, including *"Soul Man"*, by **Sam & Dave** and **Booker T. & the M.G.'s**, and *"Dock of the Bay"*, by **Otis Redding**. Also check out **Jerry Jemmott's** soulful bass line in the classic hit *"The Thrill is Gone"*, by **B.B. King**.

You can manipulate your bass to blend with any genre in so many ways. Use techniques like adjusting your warmth and depth, choosing between fingerstyle playing and picking, using different types of strings, setting your amp and EQ settings accordingly, or using minimal effects. When I had my ten-year contract developing music for *Yamaha Corporation of America,* we learned how to listen to a recording and tell what type of bass was used and what effects or style was used on each recording, and then we duplicated that sound to the best of our ability. It's incredible how close you can come as you develop your ear to hear the bass in a recording. The more you learn to blend into the style of music you are playing, the easier it becomes to collaborate with other musicians.

CHAPTER SEVEN
COLLABORATING WITH OTHER MUSICIANS

"It's very difficult sometimes having bands, you know, when all the members aren't on the same page." – Stanley Clarke

Stanley Clarke with George Duke
Credit- Wikimedia Commons

E arly in my career, back in the "big hair" days of 1980s rock, I assembled a band with an outstanding guitarist-vocalist. We sounded incredible on stage, blending perfectly. Our performance, stage presence, and vocals were stellar, and people started comparing us to the major stars of the day, like **Hall & Oates.** I firmly believe that we could have made it to colossal stardom, except for the fact that he quickly became impossible to work with. He had bipolar disorder, and one night, in a fit of feigned rage, he walked off the stage. Early on, I learned that finding musicians who are a pleasure to work with, on and off the stage, is critical. I was fortunate after that experience to find and work with legendary players, and it all came out of that early experience. People quickly learn if you are challenging to work with or unreliable, and your options get fewer. Be an excellent player, even better friend and collaborator, and you'll be a first-call musician.

SECTION ONE
JAMMING AND REHEARSING WITH BANDS

First and foremost, show up on time with decent, working equipment and a good attitude. Make sure you have extra strings and a tuned bass. A professional band is much different than a garage band. Immediately, you'll find you're going to need effective communication, tight rhythmic collaboration, and a solid understanding of improvisation.

COMMUNICATING WITH BAND MEMBERS

Verbal and Nonverbal Cues: Discuss the song structure, key changes, and dynamics before you start playing. Eye contact and body language is something you will naturally develop with your band members during live performances or jams to signal transitions, tempo changes, or endings.

Harmonizing and Listening: Pay attention to what other musicians are playing, especially the guitarist and keyboardist. The bass is the harmonic and rhythmic bridge, so knowing where to accent specific beats or complement the chord changes helps create a unified sound. For example, complementing syncopated rhythms played by other instruments can add depth to the groove in jazz or funk. Listen to the entire band, not just the drummer, to find your place in the musical conversation.

LOCKING IN WITH THE DRUMMER

Locking into the Groove: The rhythm section, consisting of the bass and drums, is the backbone of any band. To lock in with the drummer, focus on syncing with the **kick drum**. The kick drum usually defines the pulse, while the bass supports and reinforces it by playing in sync or slightly off it for variation.

Adjusting to Drum Patterns: The drummer's hi-hat and snare patterns can also inform your rhythmic approach. Pay attention to how these elements create syncopation or maintain a steady rhythm and adapt your bassline accordingly.

Feel and Dynamics: Match the **dynamics** of the drummer, whether it's a softer groove during a verse or an intense, driving rhythm for a chorus. Feeling the drummer's energy and adjusting your playing in real time will keep the band tight. Communicate with the drummer to understand their playing style and adapt your bass lines to lock in rhythmically and dynamically.

IMPROVISING

Know the Key and Chord Structure: Understanding the key and chord structure allows you to build improvised lines that fit harmonically with the other instruments. Start by outlining the chord tones (root, third, fifth, seventh) and gradually incorporate passing notes or scalar runs.

Rhythmic Freedom: Improvisation isn't just about notes but also rhythm. Use syncopation, rests, and varied note lengths to create dynamic, engaging bass lines. In funk and jazz, rhythmic improvisation can involve off-beat accents and ghost notes to add groove and depth to the jam.

Call and Response: Improvisation is a musical conversation. Listen to what everyone else is playing and respond accordingly. For example, if the guitarist plays a short melodic riff, you can echo it or play a complementary bassline, creating a dynamic and interactive jam. Start with simple, solid patterns and slowly incorporate more complex improvisation as you feel comfortable with the groove and structure.

COMPOSITION AND SONGWRITING involves crafting original bass lines, collaborating with other musicians, and understanding how the bass fits into a song's overall arrangement.

COMPOSING ORIGINAL BASS PARTS
Understand the Chord Progressions: Start by analyzing the song's harmony. Knowing the chords allows you to select notes that complement the progression.

Use Scales and Arpeggios: Incorporate notes from relevant scales (major, minor, pentatonic) and arpeggios to create melodic and cohesive bass lines.

Focus on Rhythm: Develop grooves that lock in with the drummer. Pay attention to the rhythmic patterns and syncopation to make your bass line compelling.

Balancing Simplicity and Complexity: A simple bass line sometimes serves the song best. Add complexity where appropriate, but avoid overplaying.

Experiment with Techniques: Utilize slides, hammer-ons, pull-offs, and harmonics to add character and expression to your bass lines.

Listen to Influences: Study bassists from various genres to gather ideas and inspiration for your compositions.

COLLABORATIVE SONGWRITING
Open Communication: Share ideas openly and be receptive to feedback. Collaboration thrives on mutual respect and active listening.

Jam Sessions: Engage in improvisational sessions to generate new ideas organically, leading to unexpected and exciting musical developments.

Define Roles: Understand each member's strengths and how they contribute to the group's sound. This clarity helps in creating cohesive music.

Record Rehearsals: Document your sessions to capture spontaneous ideas that can be refined later.

Flexible Adaptation: Adjust your bass parts to better suit the evolving song. Flexibility is key to effective collaboration.

Collective Decision-Making: Involve all members in the songwriting process, ensuring that everybody feels invested in the final product.

HOW BASS FITS INTO A COMPOSITION
Foundation of Harmony and Rhythm: Recognize that the bass bridges the rhythmic elements (drums) and harmonic elements (guitars, keyboards).

Dynamic Support: Adjust your playing to support different song sections. Use softer dynamics during verses and more intensity during choruses.

Complementary Playing: Avoid clashing with other instruments by choosing bass lines that fill sonic spaces without overcrowding the mix.

Textural Variation: Use the bass's different registers (low, mid, high) to add depth and variation to the arrangement.

Thematic Development: Introduce motifs or recurring patterns that enhance the song's identity and memorability.

Awareness of Song Structure: Understand the intro, verses, choruses, bridges, and outros to place your bass lines appropriately within the song's framework.

"Play as much as you can as often as you can with as many people as you can. That's how you learn and grow." – Les Claypool

Les Claypool

Credit – Scott Penner/Creativecommons.org

SECTION TWO
PLAYING IN SMALL GROUPS

As a solo performer, I naturally fill in many "holes" other band members would otherwise fill. In a group setting, I'm always aware of the other musician's contributions to the whole, and I focus on giving them the space to add to the ensemble without cacophony. Playing in small groups requires you to be foundational and flexible as a bassist.

BALANCING THE SOUND IN SMALL GROUPS

Filling the Sonic Space: The bassist provides harmonic and rhythmic support in smaller ensembles. In trios, especially, you might need to take on a more melodic role when the guitarist or pianist is soloing, like creating more elaborate lines or using double stops (playing two notes at once) to fill the harmonic gaps.

Simplifying When Needed: In quartets, where there may be more instrumental interplay, pull back and focus on simpler, driving rhythms to allow other instruments to shine, especially when dealing with complex chord progressions or when multiple instruments are soloing.

Complement the Solos: While supporting solos, keep the low end simple. Anchor the rhythm by playing straightforward, foundational basslines while leaving space for melodic and harmonic exploration by the soloists. Always be mindful of the overall texture. Remember, small groups require each member to adjust their playing to balance rhythmic support and harmonic content.

LISTENING IN REAL-TIME

Active Listening: In a small ensemble, every instrument is more exposed, and there is no room for you to "ride along." Adapt to tempo, dynamics, and phrasing shifts, constantly paying attention to the other musicians and adjusting your playing to fit their direction.

Respond to Rhythmic and Harmonic Cues: Pay attention to subtle changes in rhythm or harmony. If the drummer shifts to a new groove, lock in by adjusting your bass line accordingly. Similarly, adjust your bassline to stay harmonically aligned if the pianist or guitarist alters the harmonic progression or adds a reharmonization. Doing this can be a big task when working with a master player because the chord changes can go anywhere. It's ok not to play for a moment when you need to adjust. Fills and ghost notes sometimes work, too, when you're unsure. You anticipate what might come next as you work more often together.

Interactive Playing: Engage in musical conversations with the other musicians. For example, if the guitarist plays a rhythmic figure, you can respond with a syncopated bassline that complements their phrase, making the ensemble more cohesive and dynamic. Stay flexible. You might have to approach it differently based on the cues you get from your bandmates. This constant adjustment creates a more engaging and unified performance.

SHIFTING DYNAMICS WHEN NECESSARY

Volume Control: Managing dynamics is one of the most important aspects of playing in a small ensemble. During solos, bring down the volume of your bassline to allow the soloist to be heard clearly. Play lighter with your fingers or mute the strings slightly. When the solo ends and the band returns to a full sound, gradually kick back to full volume and intensity.

Supportive Playing: Keep a smooth, even tone in verses or quiet sections. Support the melody without overpowering it. During choruses or climaxes, your bass can become more prominent, playing more intensely to drive the group's energy.

Gradual Dynamics: Dynamics should shift naturally. For example, if the drummer increases intensity, follow their lead by gradually adding more attack to your notes or playing slightly busier lines to match the energy. Dynamics and subtle changes have a significant impact. Use dynamic shifts to help guide the song's structure and mood, ensuring smooth transitions between solos, verses, and choruses.

Dynamic shifts are great but getting louder and louder without bringing the volume back down here and there is an audience killer. Make your performances breathe. In my early career, I worked with some players who gradually turned up their volume throughout the night until it was too loud. Eventually, out of frustration, the other band members would match or exceed that volume. I love great guitarists, but most of the time, the guitarist was the culprit in these situations, turning up their amp first. Don't fall into this trap!

Remember, the most important thing when playicliffng with other musicians is for you to love the experience and look forward to the next one! My old friend, iconic entertainer **Trini Lopez** had a string of hits, and he was a favorite of **President John F. Kennedy**. Trini said:

"Everything is attitude. It's very important to always like what you're doing."

Tad Sisler with Trini Lopez
Source – Sisler Private Collection

SECTION THREE
ORCHESTRAL PLAYING

In orchestral performances, the double bass supports the harmonic and rhythmic foundation of the ensemble. Imagine a thunderous orchestra without the bottom end of the spectrum of sound! The bass literally makes the orchestra complete.

FITTING INTO AN ORCHESTRA

Supporting the Harmony: In an orchestra, the double bass often provides the foundational harmonic structure, especially in collaboration with the cello section. Bassists typically follow the low-end harmonic progression, reinforcing the root of the chords played by the rest of the orchestra.

Rhythmic Precision: The bass section in an orchestra maintains rhythmic clarity. Bassists must stay rhythmically tight, especially in large ensembles where slight timing discrepancies can disrupt the overall cohesion.

Bow Technique (Arco): Use smooth, controlled bow strokes to blend seamlessly with other sections. The right balance of bow pressure and speed produces a clean, resonant sound that supports the ensemble without overpowering it. As both a harmonic and rhythmic foundation, your role is to support the entire ensemble without becoming too prominent.

DYNAMICS AND BLENDING

Blending with Strings: Bassists work closely with cellists in the string section, often doubling parts an octave lower. Match the cellos in phrasing, articulation, and dynamics to achieve a seamless blend, maintaining a warm, rich tone through controlled bowing.

Blending with Brass and Woodwinds: When brass or woodwinds are prominent, adjust your dynamics to ensure you don't overpower these sections. Brass instruments often project powerfully, so the bass must find a balance by playing with a clear but controlled volume.

Dynamic Sensitivity: Orchestras frequently use dynamic contrasts, from pianissimo (very soft) to fortissimo (very loud). Adjust your playing accordingly. Maintain consistency in tone at all volume levels, through control of bow speed and pressure, and by varying finger pressure for pizzicato sections. Use dynamic sensitivity to support and blend with the other sections without overshadowing them.

"A good bassist determines the direction of any band. – Ron Carter

Ron Carter
Credit – Wikimedia Commons

FOLLOWING A CONDUCTOR

Watching the Conductor: Be highly attentive to the conductor's cues. These cues dictate tempo, dynamics, and articulation throughout the performance. The conductor's beat patterns are used for rhythmic precision, while hand gestures and facial expressions can signal dynamic changes and phrasing nuances.

Leading Transitions: In sections where the bass leads into key transitions or climaxes, the conductor often gives specific cues to guide these moments. Maintain eye contact and follow these cues carefully to ensure smooth transitions.

Reacting to Changes: Orchestral performances may require on-the-fly adjustments because of changes in tempo, dynamics, or phrasing. Be adaptable and ready to react to subtle gestures from the conductor to maintain the performance's cohesion. The conductor's cues are the primary guide for tempo and dynamics. Stay engaged and responsive to every gesture to ensure a unified performance.

To determine the direction of a band, master musicians are always prepared for any performance situation.

CHAPTER EIGHT
PREPARING FOR LIVE PERFORMANCES

In a recent magazine interview with **Sandy Beales,** bassist for **One Direction,** the bassist mentioned that his greatest preparation was making sure his technique was solid, with a versatile skill set, starting with mastering the bass guitar and understanding different music styles. He also focused on connecting with fellow musicians, especially drummers, since a tight rhythm section is critical for a successful performance.

Louis Tomlinson and Sandy Beales
Credit – Wikimedia Commons

Beales thinks of himself as a chameleon, able to fit into any style or situation. He also emphasizes the importance of saying 'yes' to every opportunity that comes your way, especially early in your career, because experience is the most important thing you need to succeed. He points out that playing alongside seasoned musicians helped build confidence and improve his timing, feel, and knowledge of various genres.

SECTION ONE
REHEARSING FOR PERFORMANCES

Simulating a live show during practice is an excellent way to build comfort, confidence, and endurance for actual performances. Here's how to effectively practice as though it's a live performance:

BUILD A SETLIST

Choose a setlist that mirrors a live performance regarding energy, dynamics, and style. Consider starting with something upbeat to engage the "audience" (even if imaginary) and ending with a strong closer. In my "dance band" days, we had a formula of starting a set with a showstopper, following it with a rock and roll song, doing a ballad, and then slamming many great dance covers to keep the audience engaged. Pay attention to the flow of your setlist. Include a mix of faster and slower songs, making sure they transition smoothly from one to another to keep the energy balanced. Simulate how you'd adjust your playing depending on crowd energy or audience interaction during the show. Reading a crowd is the most critical skill a band leader needs.

TRANSITIONS BETWEEN SONGS

A live performance is more than playing songs back-to-back; transitions should be smooth and deliberate. Practice transitioning between songs with minimal downtime by tuning, adjusting tone settings, or using short licks to link songs. If you plan to address the audience between songs, practice your talking points or how you'll interact with the crowd. This helps you avoid awkward silences or rushed transitions. Be real! Don't be fake or cocky. Make the audience like you by being genuine. Treat transitions as part of the performance, working on how you switch between songs and handle any potential gaps.

ENDURANCE AND STAMINA

Play your entire setlist without breaks, simulating the length and pacing of a real show. Doing this will build physical endurance, especially for your fingers and hands, while mentally preparing you to stay focused throughout a complete performance. Pay attention to how you use energy during faster or more demanding sections, and balance it with smoother, less intense songs to avoid fatigue.

Time your setlist and rehearse it for the exact length you expect in a real show to build stamina and prevent fatigue during the actual performance. Be prepared to change your setlist with additional material depending on how the crowd reacts.

MENTAL PREPARATION

Before and during your practice, visualize yourself on stage. Imagine the venue, the lights, and the audience. This mental exercise can reduce stage fright by familiarizing yourself with the feeling of being in front of a crowd. If possible, simulate live conditions, like practicing in a larger space, standing up, and playing at gig volume levels to recreate the feel of a live show. Close your eyes and envision the setting while playing—think about audience interaction, stage setup, and any movements you'll make.

FINE-TUNING YOUR PERFORMANCE

In live shows, there might be specific cues, such as when to start or stop, dynamic changes, or improvisational sections. Practice these thoroughly, especially if you're playing with a band or ensemble. In the book I wrote with legendary trumpeter **Steve Madaio**, *"Reflections In the Key of Life"*, **Steve** mentioned that when he was touring with the **Rolling Stones, Mick Jagger** built-in cues that only the band understood: if he touched his ear or moved his handkerchief, each subtle action was a cue for the band to change places, or end the song, or any number of other dynamics. If any song has a unique live arrangement (e.g., extended solo sections, different endings), practice those specific changes. Knowing these variations well will help avoid confusion during the performance. If playing with a band, make sure to communicate clearly with other musicians to sync up with these cues perfectly.

"To me, a sure-fire way to get in a rut is by sitting around playing by yourself for too long. You've gotta get out there and jam, man! You don't have to necessarily be in a band, all you've gotta have are a couple of buds who play too. They don't have to be guitarists either; jamming with a bassist or a drummer is cool." –
Dimebag Darrell

Dimebag Darrell
Credit – Wikimedia Commons

SECTION TWO
STAGE PRESENCE AND ENGAGEMENT

I've never been entirely comfortable with ten or fifty or five thousand eyes staring at me when I perform. It's hard not to think everyone is judging me or someone doesn't like me. I always do my best to connect on some level with everyone, and some gigs are better than others. I've developed some techniques that seem to help.

"I learned everything from my friends and just constant gigging in night clubs, eight sets a night! – Jaco Pastorius

CONNECTING WITH THE AUDIENCE

As a bassist, your role is often supportive, but with the right techniques, you can take center stage. Developing charisma and effectively engaging the crowd through stage presence, eye contact, body language, audience interaction, and your general demeanor cannot only enhance your performance but also create a memorable experience for your audience. In some of my performances, I really thought I wasn't reaching people, and I was surprised how many came to me afterward and told me how very much they loved the energy, song selection, and quality of my music. You never know, but remember, music is vibrational, and it touches people on many levels. Especially the bass!

"With bass, especially bottom end, the vibration has to happen on stage otherwise the feel is wrong. This is why you can't scale the equipment down too far." – John Entwistle

John Entwistle
Credit – Wikimedia Commons

STAGE MOVEMENT

Knowing when to move around the stage and when to stay still can enhance the performance's visual appeal. During energetic sections or choruses, move towards the front of the stage or interact with other band members.

Staying still can create a focused, dramatic effect for more intimate or slower moments. Use movement sparingly; constant movement can be distracting. Instead, let your movements match the mood and intensity of the music. Practice stage movement during rehearsals to feel more comfortable navigating the stage without disrupting your playing.

MAKING EYE CONTACT with people in the audience can create a personal connection. Instead of staring at your instrument or the ground, occasionally look into the crowd and make eye contact with different sections. Eye contact with the audience draws them in and helps you project confidence. Even if it feels unnatural at first, practice looking up during rehearsals. I always focus on different people during different songs to make as many in the audience feel connected to the performance as possible.

BODY LANGUAGE

For upbeat songs, use more open and dynamic gestures like head nods, foot tapping, or swaying to the rhythm. When you're playing ballads, a calm posture communicates focus and connection with the music. Stand tall, avoid slouching, and use open body language to communicate confidence.

Confident body language makes your performance more captivating. Rehearse how you stand and move with your instrument so that these gestures feel natural on stage.

AUDIENCE INTERACTION

Between songs, speak to the audience to introduce tracks, express excitement, or thank them for being there. Short comments can make the crowd feel involved without interrupting the flow of the performance. Non-verbal interaction, like smiling, nodding, or clapping along with the crowd, encourages audience participation. These small gestures invite the crowd to engage and respond to your energy. A simple smile or a thumbs-up can break the barrier between the performer and the audience.

TRANSCRIBING AND LEARNING FROM RECORDINGS provide bassists with invaluable opportunities to enhance their musical abilities and deepen their understanding of the instrument. Firstly, **transcribing** bass lines from recordings sharpens a bassist's ear training and aural skills. This practice involves listening to music to identify notes, rhythms, articulations, and dynamics. By dissecting and replicating the work of accomplished bassists, you improve your ability to recognize intervals, chord progressions, and rhythmic patterns by ear, essential for improvisation and playing in ensemble settings without relying solely on written notation.

Learning from recordings exposes you to various playing styles, techniques, and genres. This broadens your musical vocabulary and inspires creativity.

You can incorporate new techniques such as slap bass, tapping, or unique phrasing into your playing by studying different artists. Additionally, understanding how bass lines function within various musical contexts enhances your ability to compose original parts and collaborate effectively with other musicians. Transcribing and learning from recordings are powerful tools for personal growth, helping you develop a unique style and become a more versatile and expressive bassist.

Even if you're feeling nervous, remember that confidence is key. Nervous energy can be channeled into your performance, helping you stay sharp and focused. By keeping your focus on the music and the interaction with the audience, rather than worrying about mistakes or overthinking, you can project confidence and trust in your practice, making you feel more prepared and self-assured. Depending upon the venue, you will learn how to approach your performance. Nightclubs and bars can be more laid-back than private events, for instance.

CORPORATE EVENTS

Performing at corporate events, private parties, weddings, and special occasions with a band can be a lucrative way to make money on a full-time basis. Agencies, companies, and individuals hire musicians to provide live entertainment for their events, offering opportunities for paid performances and networking with potential collaborators and clients. When I started out doing this, I hooked up with an agent who controlled the corporate entertainment of several of the large hotels and convention centers in my area. Because of the number of conventions and private events agents booked for me regularly, I could quit my regular gig and work full-time doing corporate and private parties. It was a lot of setting up and breaking down my equipment, but every night was a different vibe, and I also worked many day events. The financial security and variety of opportunities are advantageous.

HOW TO HANDLE CORPORATE EVENTS

Create a checklist of all equipment, instruments, wires, stands, microphones, speakers, computers, and anything else you need for the gig. You don't want to show up without an essential instrument or stand. Eventually, you'll only need a mental checklist. After breaking down our equipment at the end of each gig, we do what we call the "idiot check," going back and checking around and under the stage for anything we might have missed. Early arrival at events is crucial. It not only provides you with sufficient time to set up your equipment and address any unforeseen issues but also reassures the event planner. Remember, people tend to arrive early, so be ready to perform at least 15 minutes before your scheduled start time. Watch your volume, especially during cocktail hours and dinner sets when people like to talk. Always look your best. Grooming and proper dress are essential for corporate gigs. Be accommodating and classy. Attitudes and emotions power everything you do. Do not eat food or drink alcohol unless the client specifically approves it. Always choose appropriate music for the moment.

Don't take long breaks unless it fits within the client's schedule. I was working a nightclub gig with a trio in **Palm Springs,** and it was a prolonged night, so we took an exceptionally long break. My saxophonist **Pat Rizzo** looked at me and said, *"We'd better go back and play. It's almost time for our next break!"* I loved that joke, but I promise clients and bar owners always look at the time and expect you to take regular breaks. Most musicians play sets of 45 minutes to an hour. The usual break time is fifteen minutes. I've done nights where the client asked in advance for continuous music without breaks, and that's what they get from me. I charged accordingly.

SECTION THREE
DEALING WITH STAGE FRIGHT

It's so important to me to make the music right that I didn't have time to be intimidated." – Marcus Miller

Marcus Miller
Credit – Wikimedia Commons

OVERCOMING PERFORMANCE ANXIETY
So many musicians turn to drugs and alcohol to calm nerves and reduce fear. The sad truth is that doing this makes it worse over time, because now you're also dealing with addiction. Always use positive means to achieve your goals whenever possible.

MINDFULNESS TECHNIQUES
Stay Focused on the Music: Focus entirely on the present moment. Concentrate on the physical sensations of playing—your fingers on the strings, the rhythm, and the sound of the music. Focusing helps prevent your mind from wandering to anxious thoughts.

Embrace the Flow: Accept that some nerves are natural. Instead of trying to avoid anxiety, acknowledge it without judgment and return your focus to your playing. Stay present to prevent overthinking. Practice mindfulness techniques off-stage through meditation or simple awareness exercises so you can apply them while performing.

BREATHING EXERCISES

Diaphragmatic Breathing: Deep breathing, also called **diaphragmatic breathing**, calms your nervous system and increases oxygen flow. Before the performance, inhale slowly through your nose for 4 counts. Hold your breath for 4 counts. Exhale slowly for 6-8 counts. Steady, focused breathing lowers your heart rate and reduces physical symptoms of anxiety.

Breathing During the Performance: Continue focusing on your breath during the show. If you feel nerves building, take a few deep breaths to return to a calm, centered state. Deep breathing can become a natural response during stressful situations.

POSITIVE VISUALIZATION

Picture Success: Mentally rehearse a successful performance. Before the show, close your eyes and visualize yourself on stage, playing confidently and the audience reacting positively. Imagine every detail, from the lights to the sound of your bass, creating a mental blueprint of success.

Reinforce Confidence: Repeating this mental rehearsal helps build confidence and familiarity with the performance environment, reducing the uncertainty that fuels anxiety. Make positive visualization a regular part of your preparation routine leading to the performance.

PROGRESSIVE RELAXATION

Progressive Muscle Relaxation: This technique involves tensing and relaxing different muscle groups to release physical tension. Starting from your toes and working up to your head, make each muscle group tense for 5-10 seconds, then relax. Doing this can be especially helpful if anxiety causes physical tightness or stiffness. I had a friend who played bass for a headliner show at a large casino in Lake Tahoe. Because the band was in the pit and the audience could not see him, he laid on his back during the entire show, playing bass flawlessly in the most relaxed position you can imagine.

Pre-show Routine: Incorporate progressive relaxation into your pre-show routine, either at home or backstage, to enter the performance in a relaxed, focused state. Combine progressive relaxation with deep breathing for maximum relaxation before a performance.

POST-PERFORMANCE SELF REFLECTION

Reflect Positively: After the performance, reflect on what went well.

Focus on the positive aspects first—what you enjoyed about the performance, what went smoothly, and how you connected with the music and the audience. **Identify Areas for Growth**: Once you've highlighted the positives, think about areas where you can improve for next time. Approach these with a growth mindset, viewing them as opportunities for learning rather than failures. Journaling your performances can also help track progress and reflect on how you're overcoming anxiety over time.

In addition to mindfulness techniques, physical actions like recording yourself and using technology can help immensely to improve your performance.

CHAPTER NINE
RECORDING AND USING TECHNOLOGY TO IMPROVE PERFORMANCE

ARTIST SPOTLIGHT:
CAROL KAYE

Carol Kaye is a legendary American bassist and one of the most prolific session musicians ever. Born on March 24, 1935, she began her music career as a jazz guitarist in the 1950s but transitioned to bass in the 1960s, where she found her true calling. **Kaye** was a vital member of the **Wrecking Crew**, a group of elite session musicians, recording on scores of the biggest hits of the 1960s and 1970s. Over her career, her iconic bass lines appeared on thousands of hit records, working with artists like **The Beach Boys**, **Simon & Garfunkel**, **Ray Charles**, and **Frank Sinatra**.

One of **Kaye's** first major sessions was on **The Righteous Brothers'** hit *"You've Lost That Lovin' Feelin'"* in 1964. This session propelled her career, establishing her as a go-to bassist for major producers like **Phil Spector**. The distinctive bassline she played not only helped set the tone for her career but also showcased her ability to bring both precision and creativity to any recording. Her work on that track, with its unique and innovative bassline, contributed to **Spector's** famous *"Wall of Sound"* technique.

Kaye's contribution to *"You've Lost That Lovin' Feelin'"* and hundreds of other major hits of the 1960s quickly elevated her status within the recording industry. From then on, she became an essential part of the Los Angeles session scene, playing on iconic albums like **The Beach Boys'** *Pet Sounds* and numerous **Motown** records. Her influence on pop, rock, and jazz bass playing is immeasurable, and she remains an icon in the music world. Even after she retired from studio work and moved to the California desert outside of Palm Springs, she remained dedicated to the next generation of musicians, serving as an influential mentor to aspiring bassists.

Kaye's career helped redefine the role of the bassist, turning it into a creative force in popular music arrangements. Through their *YouTube* tutorials, other artists have made it easy for you to study her iconic arrangements for a crash course in 20th-century bass techniques. It's not a stretch to say that **Carol Kaye** and, later, **Leland Sklar,** had the 1960s and 1970s locked up for bassists in major studios, adding their signature sound to literally hundreds of hit records.

As the leader of **The Righteous Brothers**, my friend, **Bill Medley**, recorded the hit *"You've Lost That Lovin' Feelin'"* with **Carole Kaye** on bass. He spoke about how that song and the style that came out of it, which was groundbreaking at the time.

"For Bobby and I to sing R&B and sound black was probably the stupidest thing we could do. White radio stations wouldn't play us because they thought we were black. Black stations wouldn't play us because they thought we were white. Any time you break ground, you go against the grain."

As you progress in your career, break new ground, expand your limits, and find new sounds and techniques to pass on to the next generation.

Tad Sisler with the Righteous Brothers
Source – Sisler Private Collection

SECTION ONE
SETTING UP A RECORDING SPACE
"Every note has to come out clean." – Carole Kaye

I've recorded in countless studios, from the old 1-inch reels in 8-track studios, through the 2-inch reels in 24-track studios, through the digital audio tape era, and into the DAW/Audio Interface era. I currently work on Pro Tools, but many friends prefer Logic or similar computer-based recording platforms. No matter where I recorded, ensuring the engineer captured the sound with precision and quality was the most important element. Today, almost anyone can afford to assemble a quality studio, creating recordings that rival the huge facilities if you learn it right.

ESSENTIAL EQUIPMENT
Audio Interface: The first crucial piece of equipment is a high-quality audio interface. Look for one with **high headroom** and **low-latency** performance to handle the low frequencies of your bass. Popular options as I write this book include **Focusrite Scarlett, Universal Audio Apollo,** or **PreSonus Audiobox.** Ensure the interface has **multiple inputs** if you plan to record simultaneously through a **direct input (DI)** and microphone.

Microphones: Use a combination of microphones depending on the type of bass you are recording. A **dynamic microphone** (like the **Shure SM57**) works well for electric bass when placed close to the amp. Use **large-diaphragm condenser microphones** (such as the **AKG C414** or **Neumann U87**) for upright bass or contrabass to capture more tonal depth and resonance. Today, a bassist can record directly into the interface if desired, recording clean or using many plugins to simulate amps and effects. I like to achieve both at the same time, with a clean bass track next to the mic'd amp track. This flexibility can be helpful later if I want to add effects or double a synth using the clean track. Ensure your interface has **phantom power** for condenser microphones.

"In the studio, I don't use an amp, I just go direct into the desk. It's virtually acoustic, what I'm doing." – Jaco Pastorius

Headphones: Invest in high-quality, closed-back headphones like **Audio-Technica ATH-M50X** or **Beyerdynamic DT 770 Pro** to avoid sound bleed into your recordings and accurately monitor your bass sound.

ACOUSTIC TREATMENT
Foam Panels and Bass Traps: Acoustic foam panels help absorb reflections and reduce room reverb, making the recording more controlled.

Place **bass traps** in the corners to keep the lower frequencies from muddying up the bass sound.

These capture clean, deep tones without excessive bass buildup in untreated rooms.

Carpets or Curtains: Using carpets or heavy curtains can help minimize reflective surfaces, creating a more neutral recording environment. Carpets, particularly beneath amps or recording setups, help prevent sound waves from bouncing off hard floors. Try to eliminate as many hard reflective surfaces as possible. Position foam strategically around the room, especially at reflection points (walls, corners).

RECORDING SOFTWARE (DAW)

Choosing the Right DAW: Popular DAWs like **Logic Pro**, **Ableton Live**, **Pro Tools**, or **Reaper** are all user-friendly and highly effective.

Look for a DAW that suits your workflow and offers good plugin support for bass-specific effects, like compression and EQ. If you're new to recording, consider starting with **GarageBand** or **Reaper**, which are user-friendly and accessible for beginners. If you do this, however, assuming you stick to the craft of recording, you'll eventually have to graduate to a more pro DAW. Learning a new recording software platform is relatively easy, but I compare it to learning a new language. The words mean the same thing, yet they're entirely different. When I developed music for *Yamaha Corporation of America*, the job required me to work between **MOTU's Digital Performer** and my native **Pro Tools**, because, at the time, functionality worked best for me that way. It was confusing at times, especially when you learn the short-cut macros on the computer keyboard because different software has different commands to achieve the same thing.

Plugins: Look for bass-centric plugins such as **Ampeg SVX** for amp simulations or **Waves CLA Bass** for added tonal versatility. DAWs with strong plugin support allow you to experiment with different tones and effects during post-production.

MICROPHONE PLACEMENT

Electric Bass: Place the microphone close to the **center of the bass amp's speaker cone** for a bright, punchy tone and towards the **edge of the cone** for a warmer, rounder sound. Using a DI box in combination with mic'ing the amp gives you flexibility in blending clean DI tones with the amp's character.

Upright Bass and Contrabass: For upright or contrabass, place a **condenser microphone** about 12–18 inches from the **bridge** for a whole, natural tone. Alternatively, mic the **f-hole** or use two mics (one near the f-hole, another higher up the neck) to capture a balance of resonance and string articulation. Experiment with mic distance and angle. Moving the mic a few inches can change the recorded tone.

EXPERIMENTING WITH TONE

EQ Settings: Start with minimal EQ and gradually tweak as necessary. If your tone is too boomy, use a **low-cut filter** to clean up unnecessary sub-bass frequencies. Boosting the mid-range can add clarity to bass lines in a dense mix.

Amp and DI Balance: When recording electric bass, experiment with blending the **DI signal** (for clean, direct tone) and the **amp signal** (for warmth and character). Play around with different mixes to find the right balance for the song's style.

Compression: Bass often requires compression to control dynamics. Use a compressor plugin or a hardware unit with settings that focus on taming peaks without squashing the natural attack of the bass notes.

As mentioned, record multiple takes of different tones (clean, compressed, or effects-driven) to have options during post-production.

Whichever way you set up your studio, ensure you learn the craft enough to create flawless recordings. Multi-platinum artist **Snoop Dogg**, said:

"If it's flipping hamburgers at McDonald's, be the best hamburger flipper in the world. Whatever it is you do, you have to master your craft."

Snoop Dogg and Tad Sisler
Source – Sisler Private Collection

SECTION TWO
PRACTICING WITH RECORDING TOOLS

The beauty of our era is that we have so many tools to work with to improve ourselves. Scientists are finding new cures for diseases using artificial intelligence, and we have a new world at our fingertips. Leveraging AI technology in the recording studio can significantly enhance your development. Here are a few ways:

RECORD YOUR PRACTICE SESSIONS

Recording your practice sessions lets you objectively evaluate your playing and spot mistakes. Listening back helps identify timing issues, incorrect notes, or tone inconsistencies. Use your DAW to record a session and listen carefully. Focus on articulation, timing, and overall tone. Recording different versions at varying tempos can also highlight specific weak spots.

AI Enhancement: Use AI-powered apps like **Moises.ai**, which can help isolate the bass track in popular songs. Isolating your bass allows you to compare your playing with the original recordings more accurately. Also, compare your recordings with isolated basslines to understand how your timing and tone match professional recordings.

ISOLATING PARTS AND LOOPING:

Looping specific sections helps bassists focus on problematic parts of a song and work through them methodically. Select a challenging section in your DAW and loop it for repeated practice. Gradually increase the tempo as you improve.

AI Enhancement: **SmartMetronome** is an AI tool that automatically adjusts the tempo as you practice, allowing for progressive improvement without manual adjustment. AI-based tools can intelligently increase the difficulty level as you master a section.

ANALYZING YOUR TIMING

Precise timing is paramount because a bassist anchors the rhythm section. Practicing with a metronome keeps your groove tight. Use a metronome or drum loop in your DAW and record yourself playing along. Listen to how well you stay locked in with the beat.

AI Enhancement: AI tools like **Beat Mirror** or **Metronomics** offer real-time feedback on timing accuracy. These tools can track if you're rushing or dragging the beat and offer adjustments to improve your groove. Using AI rhythm trainers helps you develop more precise timing and stay in sync with other instruments.

TRACKING YOUR FINGER ACCURACY:

Sloppy or rushed finger movements can result in unclear notes or tonal inconsistencies. Recording your practice allows you to catch these issues— record videos of your finger movements or just the audio of your bass playing. Listening carefully or watching your hands can reveal rushed movements or improper finger placements.

AI Enhancement: AI tools like **Sibelius Ultimate** (with AI-powered score writing) can transcribe your playing into sheet music, allowing you to analyze your finger positions and accuracy against the score.

You can also use AI-driven software to convert your playing into sheet music, making analyzing finger movements and timing discrepancies easier.

UNDERSTANDING MIXING TECHNIQUES shows you how to bring out subtle nuances in your playing. A well-mixed bassline balances the instrument and makes it prominent. After recording, use EQ to adjust low-end frequencies, compression to even out dynamics, and reverb or other effects to add depth. I've often panned the bass guitar and the kick drum to center for a big mix while stereo-panning some bass effects to make it cool—experiment with mixing different tones.

AI Enhancement: AI-based tools like **iZotope Neutron** or **LANDR** provide AI-assisted mixing. These tools analyze your track and offer suggestions or auto-mixing features to balance frequencies, optimize compression, and enhance tonal quality.

You can also use AI-driven mixing tools to identify potential issues in your bass mix, helping you to balance your sound.

USE AI FOR PERSONAL FEEDBACK

AI tools can offer personalized, real-time feedback on various aspects of your playing. Use AI platforms like **Moises.ai** or **Sibelius Ultimate** to isolate bass parts, analyze timing, and provide feedback on your playing. Check out my section on multiple AI tools in this book.

KEYBOARD BASS IN THE STUDIO AND ONSTAGE

After years of recording and performing, I've become an extremely proficient keyboard bass player. Having said that, I know only too well that there is never a substitute for the actual bass, played by a master player, that can come close to any keyboard bass. However, synth bass is popular in genres like pop, EDM, funk, and hip-hop, allowing you to craft deep, sub-heavy tones or more aggressive mid-range bass lines. Synth bass can range from fat, analog sounds to sharp, punchy electronic bass lines. Why not embrace and learn how to play a killer synth bass on a keyboard while learning to master the bass, in case you find yourself in a situation that requires it? You can experiment with different oscillators, filters, and envelopes to create unique bass sounds to fit your track's needs.

KEYBOARD BASS TECHNIQUES

There may be riffs you can play on keyboard bass that are physically impossible to play on a bass guitar. I say "maybe" because I've seen some monster performances from musicians that I previously thought were impossible!

I learned keyboard bass techniques from some of the best bassists and keyboard bassists.

Gilbert Hansen showed me blues riffs on his bass guitar, and he also used a staccato bass on R&B ballads when returning to the verse for emotive effect. **Dennis Michaels** had such a solid left hand on the keyboard; his playing inspired me to learn how fast you can play an upright bass track on swing tunes. **Craig Eaton** was a classic rock pianist and left-handed keyboard bass player who hit every bass note twice on fast classic rock tunes. **Lonnie Reaves** produced one of my projects, and his smooth, effortless, quick, and dissonant R&B lines were so cool that I incorporated them into my style. **Joe Vanelli, Gino Vanelli's** brother, and **Leon Gaer** played most of the incredible synth keyboard bass on **Gino's** recordings (when **Gino** wasn't using legendary bassist **Jimmy Haslip** or **Damian Erskine** on bass guitar). **Vanelli** was among the first to combine synth bass with bass guitar on recordings, including the verse/chorus trade-off on his masterpiece *"The River Must Flow."*

For a crash course on emulating the most iconic synth or key bass parts, you can study iconic bass parts on *"I Feel Love"* by **Donna Summer**, *"Chameleon"* by **Herbie Hancock**, *"Superstition"* by **Stevie Wonder**, *"Let's Dance"* by **David Bowie**, *"Good Times"* by **Chic**, *"Billie Jean"* by **Michael Jackson**, *"1999"* by **Prince**, *"Blue Monday"* by **New Order**, and *"Radioactive"* by **Imagine Dragons**. Learning these techniques will also help your approach to bass guitar when playing specific genres.

[Side note: When I was writing **Steve Madaio's** award-winning biography with him, entitled *"Reflections in the Key of Life,"* **Steve** mentioned that only three players performed on the **Stevie Wonder** #1 Smash hit song *"Superstition."* **Stevie Wonder** played all the parts, including drums and keyboard bass, while **Trevor Lawrence** played saxophone and **Steve Madaio** played trumpet. **Madaio** told me that since only three players were on that smash #1 single, he made enough royalties to purchase a new home and could have lived comfortably on that alone for a while. All you needed back then was one smash hit, combined with touring, to be set for life.]

Jimi "Fitz" Fitzgerald, Tad Sisler, and Steve Madaio
Source – Sisler Private Collection

USING MOD WHEEL AND PITCH BEND

Mod Wheel: The mod wheel on a keyboard is often used to control the **vibrato** or **filter cutoff** on synth bass, adding expression and movement to otherwise static bass notes.

Try slowly increasing the mod wheel during a sustained note to create a dramatic filter sweep, giving the bass line more texture.

Pitch Bend: The pitch bend wheel on a keyboard is frequently used to create **slides** or **glissandos** between notes, mimicking the effect of a bass guitarist sliding between frets. Subtle pitch bends can add expressiveness to synth bass lines, making them feel more fluid and organic. Use the pitch bend wheel sparingly to avoid overdoing the effect and smooth the modulation for more natural transitions.

"I've always been a great believer that you have to keep producing new things in order to keep life interesting – not only for ourselves, but for the audience as well. That's really always been our principle and way of working." – Chris Squire

Chris Squire
Credit – Wikimedia Commons

BEST PLUGINS FOR SYNTH BASS

Arturia Mini V: A recreation of the classic Minimoog, it's known for its rich, punchy bass tones, perfect for both vintage and modern bass lines.

Serum by Xfer Records: This wavetable synthesizer is widely used for its versatility, especially in electronic genres. It allows for deep customization of bass sounds and supports modulation, filters, and effects.

Spectrasonics Trilian: Designed specifically for bass, this plugin offers a vast library of electric, acoustic, and synth bass sounds. Its realism and attention to detail make it ideal for studio bass work. Using **Trilian**, I've created entire realistic bass parts with ghost notes, fills, and bends.

Massive by Native Instruments: Known for its deep, growling bass tones, Massive is great for creating complex, powerful synth bass sounds that cut through the mix. It is often used in electronic music.

Experiment with different presets and tweak parameters like the attack, sustain, and filter settings to fit your track's genre and energy.

SECTION THREE
CREATING DEMO RECORDINGS

Recording demos is an excellent way to assess your performance and share your work with others. Always start with quality music that you believe will resonate with others.

BUILDING YOUR REPERTOIRE

When I started as a performer, I had my book of around fifty songs and continued adding songs over the years.

Today I have a repertoire of over three thousand songs I can play by ear. You don't need more than a handful to start out but having a personal portfolio of recordings showcases your versatility and technical ability. It also allows you to assess your growth over time.

Record a variety of bass lines that highlight different techniques (fingerstyle, slap, pick) and genres (rock, jazz, funk, etc.). This diversity not only showcases your skills but also opens up new possibilities for collaboration and growth. Focus on tight timing, clean articulation, and a balanced tone. Aim for polished recordings that represent your best work. These recordings can be original compositions or covers that highlight your skills. Choose songs that best represent your unique style and strengths. Make sure to have a diverse range to appeal to different audiences or collaborators.

> *"If you've got a good song, it's easy to play. But you can't make a bad song sound good no matter who you have to play on it."*
> *– Donald "Duck" Dunn*

COLLABORATING WITH OTHER MUSICIANS allows you to grow by incorporating their feedback and adjusting your performance to fit group dynamics. Share your recordings with fellow musicians or producers. You can grow quickly by using input from other musicians to refine your bass lines, groove, and overall musicality. Send them raw bass tracks to add their instruments or provide a completed demo for feedback on composition and arrangement. Tools like **Google Drive** or **Dropbox** allow easy file sharing, making it simple to collaborate remotely. I brought all the musicians I needed into my studios for years and produced and engineered their tracks.

Today, I send my **Pro Tools** sessions out to great studio musicians, and they send me back perfect parts.

USING ONLINE PLATFORMS

Uploading to online platforms increases your visibility and lets you showcase your work to a broader audience. It's also an excellent way to document progress. After recording and mixing your demo, export it in a high-quality format (WAV or MP3) and upload it to **SoundCloud**, **YouTube**, or **Bandcamp**.

Include your name, song title, contact number or email, and description in the metadata so that potential collaborators or listeners can easily find and engage with your work. Consider adding a video component, like a simple performance video, when uploading to **YouTube**, as it adds a visual element that can engage your audience more.

CROWD-SOURCING FOR FEEDBACK

Receiving feedback from a broad range of listeners can be a game-changer in your musical journey.

Online communities can provide insights that you might not get from friends or collaborators. Share your demos on forums like **Reddit's WeAreTheMusicMakers**, **Gearslutz**, or social media groups for bassists and musicians. These platforms are great for getting honest feedback on your tone, timing, and overall performance. Be open to both positive and constructive feedback and use it to enhance your technical and creative abilities. Remember, feedback is not criticism, but a steppingstone to improvement.

IDENTIFYING YOUR STRENGTHS

Reviewing your recordings helps you become more aware of areas that need improvement and reinforces your strengths. After recording, listen back to each track carefully. Focus on critical areas like **timing**, **tone**, **articulation**, and **dynamics**. Identify spots where your playing may be sloppy or rushed and compare different takes to find the best performance. Use the solo bass track (if recording with other instruments) to isolate your playing and hear your performance without distraction.

Speaking of building on strengths and overcoming weaknesses, my friend, **President George H. W. Bush**, created a list of motivating thoughts. I turn to this list occasionally, for inspiration to stay emotionally present and focused:

1. Don't get down when your life takes a bad turn. Out of adversity comes challenge and often success.

2. Don't blame others for your setbacks.

3. When things go well, always give credit to others.

4. Don't talk all the time. Listen to your friends and mentors and learn from them.

5. *Don't brag about yourself. Let others point out your virtues, your strong points.*

6. *Give someone else a hand. When a friend is hurting, show that friend you care.*

7. *Nobody likes an overbearing big shot.*

8. *As you succeed, be kind to people. Thank those who help you along the way.*

9. *Don't be afraid to shed a tear when your heart is broken because a friend is hurting.*

10. *Say your prayers!!"*

These words by President Bush might help you build a well-rounded practice routine, along with my next chapter.

President George H. W. Bush, Barbara Bush and Tad Sisler

Source – Sisler Private Collection

CHAPTER TEN
BUILDING A WELL-ROUNDED PRACTICE ROUTINE

ARTIST SPOTLIGHT
JOHN PATITUCCI

B ack in the late 1990s, in my studio in Burbank, California, I came across this great collection of bass sounds created by master bassist **John Patitucci.** In this collection, along with the sounds of **Marcus Miller** and a handful of other bassists, we could fly in and use the actual bass of the artist in the early days of DAW recording. It was a revelation at the time to do this!

John Patitucci is widely respected for his mastery of electric and upright bass. Early in his career, he created a highly disciplined practice schedule, setting aside several hours each day to focus on multiple aspects of bass playing, including:

Scales and arpeggios: To develop foundational solid technique.

Harmonic practice: To understand complex jazz harmonies and how to incorporate them into his improvisation.

Sight-reading and transcribing: To increase his versatility and musical knowledge.

This strict practice routine helped **John Patitucci** become a versatile bassist, effortlessly switching between jazz, classical, and Latin music. I love his work with **Chick Corea's Elektric Band**, and his solo projects are excellent. Because of his disciplined practice, he was able to handle complex and challenging musical situations throughout his career. Study and emulate his work to achieve your own excellence.

John Patitucci
Credit: Photo: Tore Sætre – Wikimedia Commons/CC BY-SA 4.0

SECTION ONE
SETTING REALISTIC PRACTICE GOALS

In our busy lives, the only time we find is time we make. It all begins with time management.

THE ESSENCE OF TIME MANAGEMENT

Dividing your practice time ensures that each critical area of your playing gets attention. Without a plan, it's easy to focus too much on one aspect (e.g., technique) and neglect other essential elements like rhythm or improvisation. Break down your practice into sections, such as:

Technique (20-30 mins): Focus on finger exercises, scales, and improving dexterity.

Rhythm (15-20 mins): Play along with a metronome or drum tracks, working on locking into different tempos and styles.

Improvisation (15-20 mins): Practice soloing over chord progressions or jamming to backing tracks, developing creativity.

Tailor the time spent on each section to fit your goals and needs, increasing or decreasing the time as necessary.

SETTING SPECIFIC, MEASURABLE, ACHIEVABLE, RELEVANT, AND TIME-BOUND (SMART) GOALS

SMART goals keep your practice focused and progress-driven. Instead of vague goals like "get better," SMART goals offer clarity and accountability. Break down your practice goals using the SMART method:

Specific: Set a clear goal (e.g., "learn all modes of the major scale").

Measurable: Set a way to measure success (e.g., "Play all modes at 120 BPM").

Achievable: Set a realistic goal on your current level (e.g., "Master one mode per week").

Relevant: Make sure it aligns with your broader musical goals (e.g., improving jazz improvisation).

Time-Bound: Set a deadline (e.g., "Complete all modes in one month").

Write down and review your goals regularly to stay motivated and track your progress.

TRACKING PROGRESS WITH A JOURNAL

A practice journal is a great tool for staying accountable, as well as on reflecting on what works and needs improvement. After each practice session, jot down what you worked on, what felt challenging, and any progress made. Over time, this log will provide insight into which areas need more attention or how you've improved. Include both short-term successes (e.g., "Improved my timing with a metronome") and longer-term goals (e.g., "Mastered fingerstyle technique in funk music").

ADJUSTING YOUR GOALS

Your strengths and weaknesses will evolve as you practice. Adapting your practice routine to your current needs is key to staying challenged and engaged. If a particular goal becomes too easy or too difficult, adjust it. For example, gradually increase the speed if you've mastered a particular scale at a slower tempo. If a technique is too hard, slow it down and focus on a tiny aspect until it feels more manageable. Review your journal weekly or monthly to reassess your progress and adjust goals as needed.

CONSISTENT DAILY PRACTICE

Regular, focused practice is more effective than long, sporadic sessions.

Short, daily practice sessions build muscle memory and skills steadily over time without overwhelming you. Aim for 30-60 minutes of focused practice each day rather than waiting for large blocks of time. Consistency helps you internalize techniques and concepts faster. Even on busy days, try to fit in 10-15 minutes of practice to keep the momentum going. Don't lose faith, ever! Even the masters feel frustration with themselves on occasion.

"I'm in competition with myself and I'm losing! – Roger Waters

Roger Waters
Credit – Wikimedia Commons

SECTION TWO
BALANCING TECHNIQUES, REPERTOIRE, AND PERFORMANCE SKILLS

Rotate the focus of each practice session. Changing focus is a great way to stay motivated while constantly challenging your brain to take uncharted risks.

TECHNIQUE EXERCISES AND DRILLS

Developing finger strength, accuracy, and timing is the foundation of solid bass playing. Practice scales (major, minor, modes), arpeggios, and chromatic exercises. Use a **metronome** to improve timing and incorporate **slap bass** or fingerstyle drills if they are part of your style. Incorporate AI-based rhythm trainers like **Beat Mirror** to check and fine-tune your timing during practice. **Use spider exercises** for finger independence. **Use string skipping drills** to improve agility and accuracy. **Use rhythmic drills** to sync with different time signatures.

ADDING NEW SONGS: Expanding your repertoire improves versatility and knowledge of various music styles. Break new pieces down into manageable sections. Focus on tricky parts first, and then work on stringing them together. Study bass lines from different genres (jazz, rock, funk) to broaden your skills. Use **transcription software** like **Transcribe!** or **Moises.ai** to slow the recordings and isolate the bass lines for learning.

Start slow, learning one section at a time. Focus on precision before gradually increasing speed. Play along with the original recording to match nuances in timing and dynamics.

IMPROVISATION AND CREATIVITY

Improvisation is critical to improving creativity and versatility on the bass. It helps develop musical intuition and flexibility. Practice over different chord progressions, experiment with scales and modes, and create your own basslines. Use AI tools like **Chord AI** to generate backing tracks or chord progressions to jam over, helping you practice improvisation in a musical context. Start simple, using **pentatonic scales** or **arpeggios**. Practice phrasing and rhythmic variation by playing with different note durations and accents. Record your improvisation and listen back to identify patterns or ideas you like.

REVIEWING AND PERFECTING PAST PIECE

Revisiting and polishing old songs or techniques helps reinforce learning and discover new ways to improve. Play through previously learned pieces to ensure they remain fresh and error-free. Pay attention to details like dynamics, articulation, and groove.

Record yourself playing old pieces and use AI-powered analysis tools like **Sibelius** or **Soundtrap** to get visual feedback on timing, note accuracy, and dynamics.

Focus on sections that were challenging initially. Try playing the piece with new variations (e.g., altering rhythms or changing the key)—experiment with incorporating learned techniques into older pieces.

STAYING FOCUSED AND RELAXED

Mental clarity and relaxation are crucial for effective practice and performance. Before or after a session, practice mindfulness, focusing on deep breathing or visualization to reduce anxiety and increase focus. Apps like **Headspace** or **Calm** can guide short meditative sessions that enhance your practice by helping you stay present and reducing performance anxiety.

Deep breathing: Inhale for 4 counts, hold for 4, exhale for 6.

Visualization: Picture yourself performing confidently or successfully playing a challenging section.

Body scanning: Focus on relaxing each body part, starting from your toes and moving upwards.

USE AI TOOLS FOR SELF-IMPROVEMENT

As previously mentioned, use new technology to build upon your technique, accuracy, and style.

Timing analysis: Use apps like **Beat Mirror** or **Soundbrenner** for real-time timing analysis.

Backing track generation: Tools like **Chord AI** or **iReal Pro** can create backing tracks to simulate real-band practice, enhancing your improvisation and timing.

Feedback on practice: Tools like **Yousician** or **Sibelius** offer AI feedback on your playing, helping you identify areas for improvement in real time (see our section on AI-Powered apps).

I WANT TO OFFER YOU A FREE GIFT

I hope you're loving this book so far. Learning an instrument can be daunting, but the rewards are exponential as you learn and grow your performance skills. I've created a list of **TEN SECRETS A MUSICIAN CANNOT LIVE WITHOUT,** and I want to share it with you.

If you want a free copy of my list, email us at...
<<   modernrenaissancepublishing@gmail.com   >>
with the subject line **TEN SECRETS FREE LIST,** and I'll email you back a free copy at no obligation whatsoever to you as a heartfelt thanks for reading this book.

SECTION THREE
INCORPORATING MINDFULNESS AND PSYCHOLOGICAL TECHNIQUES

THE ROLE OF MENTAL PRACTICE

Practicing without physically playing your instrument will help you grow exponentially. Many nights, as I prepare to sleep, I play changes in my head or work out a problematic passage step-by-step in a song. Combining mental focus with physical practice will accelerate progress, improve your accuracy, and build confidence.

STAYING PRESENT AND AWARE: Mindfulness helps you stay in the moment, focusing entirely on the task in front of you. It reduces distractions and enables more efficient learning.

During practice, concentrate fully on sounds, finger movements, and rhythms. Focus on feeling each exercise in your body rather than thinking about future or past mistakes. Start your practice with a short mindfulness exercise like deep breathing to center yourself, then focus intently on each aspect of the bass line you are practicing.

"People should decide what success means for them, and not be distracted by accepting others' definitions of success." – Tony Levin

Tony Levin
Credit – Wikimedia Commons

MENTAL REHEARSAL

Visualization is a powerful way to rehearse without your instrument, improving muscle memory and allowing you to mentally solve difficult passages before physically attempting them. Close your eyes and visualize your fingers moving across the fretboard or imagine playing through a tricky section of a song.

Visualize every detail: the sound, the finger positions, and even how you'll feel when you play it perfectly. Spend 5-10 minutes daily visualizing difficult sections, imagining yourself playing easily and precisely.

HANDLING FRUSTRATION:

Frustration during practice can derail progress but learning to stay calm and patient ensures continuous improvement. When you feel frustrated, pause and take a few deep breaths. Acknowledge the feeling but refocus on the small progress you've already made. Break down the challenging section into smaller, more manageable parts, and celebrate minor improvements. Remember that every musician faces challenges, and that consistent, small progress will lead to mastery.

USING POSITIVE SELF-TALK

Positive self-talk can reframe your mindset, boost confidence, and help you push through difficult practice sessions.

Instead of saying, **"I can't do this,"** try saying, **"I'm improving each time I play this section,"** or **"I'll get better with practice."** Replace negative thoughts with positive, goal-oriented affirmations. Write down a few positive affirmations related to your bass playing and keep them in your practice space to reinforce confidence.

USING REPETITIVE PRACTICE
TO CREATE MUSCLE MEMORY

Repetition helps build **muscle memory** so your fingers can execute patterns and techniques with minimal conscious effort. Focus on repeatedly playing tricky passages or scales, starting slowly and gradually increasing speed as your accuracy improves. Each repetition reinforces the correct finger movements, timing, and tone control. Set a goal to play a passage 10-15 times perfectly before moving on to another section. This level of repetition creates familiarity and breeds confidence.

AVOIDING STEREOTYPES

Nathan East is one of my very favorite master bassists. As a founding member of **Fourplay,** later working with **Herbie Hancock, George Harrison, Michael Jackson, Quincy Jones,** and just about everyone else in the business, he's seen it all. **Nathan** will be the first to tell you to run in the opposite direction of stereotypes!

"In rock'n'roll, as we all know, the image is that it's one big party. But many times, the reality is that it's the furthest thing from the party. There's the alcoholism and drug abuse that come because you're looking for that elusive 'thing,' and you don't know what it is or where it is. But you've got the money and the connections, and the choices are not always the healthiest." – Nathan East

Nathan East

Credit – Flickr/Creativecommons.org

In all my music mastery books, I urge the reader to reject stereotypes. The most important thing you can do is what you don't do! Throughout my life, I've encountered people who bought into the negative stereotypes about musicians. When I mentioned that I was a musician, I would get a look from someone who immediately judged me as a loser. It's sad, but you will do all of us a favor if you exemplify yourself as a professional and never exhibit any of these negative stereotypes. My old friend, championship-winning *NFL* Quarterback, **Congressman and Secretary of Housing and Urban Development Jack Kemp** talked about it in a unique way. **Kemp** said:

"Winning is like shaving – you do it every day or you wind up looking like a bum."

Tad Sisler with Congressman Jack Kemp
Source – Sisler Private Collection

It's all about the way you carry yourself, with pride and self-respect. People will pick up on your attitudes, emotions, and habits. Be the best version of yourself always and avoid these stereotypes:

MUSICIANS ARE UNRELIABLE AND IRRESPONSIBLE – People often stereotype musicians as flaky, unreliable, and irresponsible, particularly regarding commitments and punctuality. I will immediately write anyone off my call list who can't regularly show up on time with suitable instruments and clothing for the gig.

SUBSTANCE ABUSE – There is a pervasive stereotype that musicians are prone to drug and alcohol abuse, often glamorized in media and popular culture.

FINANCIAL INSTABILITY – Although this is something we cannot always control when we commit to this industry, unfortunately, many people stereotype musicians as struggling financially, living paycheck to paycheck, or unable to support themselves through their music alone. One of my friends who regularly comes to my gig has a running joke with me. He'll say, "You're good. Have you considered doing this for a living?" And I'll say, "No, it doesn't pay enough!" Everyone laughs, but the sad truth is that many musicians are grossly underpaid for their talents. But don't let this define you.

NO PRACTICAL SKILLS – Musicians are sometimes viewed as lacking practical or marketable skills outside of their music, contributing to the idea that they have few career options.

EGO AND ARROGANCE – Musicians, especially successful ones, are often stereotyped as having big egos or arrogant, believing they are superior because of their talent. I've worked with many excellent musicians who were impossible to work with. We sounded great on stage together, but the whole experience was not worth it because of their egos or negativity. Always try to enjoy the experience and let go!

UNCONVENTIONAL LIFESTYLE – There is a stereotype that musicians lead unconventional or chaotic lifestyles with irregular hours, frequent travel, and unstable relationships.

EMOTIONAL INSTABILITY – People sometimes judge as emotionally unstable or overly sensitive, with intense mood swings or dramatic behaviour.

PROMISCUITY – Particularly in rock and pop culture, musicians are often stereotyped as promiscuous and engaging in numerous short-term relationships. Groupies don't help erase this stereotype!

NON-CONFORMITY – People often see musicians as rebels or non-conformists who reject societal norms and conventional careers.

LACK OF FORMAL EDUCATION – There's a stereotype that musicians are less formally educated or lack academic achievements, focusing solely on their craft.

These stereotypes are not universally true and can be harmful, as they overlook many musicians' diversity, dedication, and professionalism. I must admit, though, that I've often told people I'm a composer, producer, author, entertainer, or many other titles (all true) besides musician. Help propel us all forward by going against the stereotype!

TEACHING OTHERS TO PLAY BASS

Now that you've learned techniques, theory, and just about everything else you need to be a master bassist, why not teach what you know to others? For bassists interested in teaching, understanding pedagogy principles is the key to effectively sharing their knowledge and passion for the instrument. Teaching bass involves more than just demonstrating techniques; it requires communicating concepts clearly and inspiring students. Consider these aspects:

FUNDAMENTALS OF INSTRUCTION
UNDERSTAND DIFFERENT LEARNING STYLES

Visual Learners: Benefit from diagrams, charts, and written notation.
Auditory Learners: Prefer listening to explanations and musical examples.
Kinesthetic Learners: Hands-on activities and physical engagement help these students to learn their craft.

Application: Adapt your teaching methods to accommodate these styles for effective learning.

SET CLEAR OBJECTIVES

Define Goals: Establish what you and your student aim to achieve in each lesson and over time.

Structured Progression: Develop a curriculum that builds skills logically and progressively.

Master the Basics:

Technique: Emphasize proper hand positioning, finger movement, and posture.

Theory: Teach foundational music theory relevant to bass playing.

Ear Training: Incorporate exercises that develop listening skills and musical intuition.

ENCOURAGE ACTIVE PARTICIPATION

Ask Questions: Promote an interactive environment where students feel comfortable asking questions.

Provide Feedback: Offer constructive criticism and acknowledge improvements.

STRUCTURING EFFECTIVE LESSON PLANS

LESSON COMPONENTS

Warm-Up Exercises: Begin with scales, arpeggios, or finger dexterity drills.

Review Previous Material: Reinforce past lessons to ensure retention.

Introduce New Concepts: Break down complex ideas into manageable parts.

Practical Application: Use songs or improvisation to apply new skills in a musical context.

Homework Assignments: Provide precise practice tasks with specific goals.

CUSTOMIZATION

Assess Individual Needs: Tailor lessons to the student's skill level, interests, and learning pace.

Set Short-Term and Long-Term Goals: Help students stay motivated by tracking their progress.

TIME MANAGEMENT

Balance Activities: Allocate time efficiently between different lesson components.

Flexibility: Be prepared to adjust the lesson plan based on the student's comprehension and engagement.

INCORPORATE TECHNOLOGY

Use Teaching Aids: Leverage apps, online resources, and backing tracks to enhance learning.

Recording Sessions: Encourage students to record themselves to self-evaluate and track improvement.

CONVEYING COMPLEX IDEAS IN UNDERSTANDABLE WAYS

SIMPLIFY TECHNICAL CONCEPTS
Use Analogies: Relate new information to familiar concepts to make it more accessible.
Step-by-Step Explanations: Break down processes into sequential steps.

ACTIVE LISTENING
Understand Student Perspectives: Pay attention to their concerns and questions.
Adapt Communication: Modify your explanations based on the student's responses.

CLEAR AND CONCISE LANGUAGE
Avoid Jargon: Use terminology appropriately and explain new terms when introduced.
Repetition and Reinforcement: Repeat key points to reinforce learning.

ENGAGEMENT TECHNIQUES
Ask Open-Ended Questions: Stimulate critical thinking and deeper understanding.
Encourage Expression: Allow students to share their ideas and interpretations.

VISUAL DEMONSTRATIONS
Demonstrate Techniques: Show rather than tell to enhance comprehension.
Use Visual Aids: Incorporate fretboard diagrams and notation to support explanations.

CONCLUSION

The ongoing journey to mastery is full of pitfalls and extraordinary moments. It requires dedication, purpose, and mostly perseverance. Never give up! The bass, this glorious instrument, is not just a part of the musical palate; it is the bottom end, backbone, and foundation. Your role as a bass player is unique and invaluable. Playing bass gives you a powerful feeling. Playing nuances, complementing, and accenting songs is an art form reserved for a select few, and you are one of them.

"I think the future looks great for music, musicians, bass players, and all we love about music." — Billy Sheehan

Billy Sheehan
Credit – Mr. Big/Wikimedia Commons

My journey has been a blessing, allowing me to perform with the very best and produce the finest music. I've had the honor of witnessing great players leave their mark on my music. It's often said that a photograph is a mirror with a memory. In the same way, a recording or performance is a musical moment that nobody can ever take from you. It becomes a part of your memory and your personal mental soundtrack forever. Keep setting new goals, learning, and refining your skills. View this journey as continuous growth, knowing each musical moment you create will live on in memory.

And finally, thank you so much for your commitment to bass playing. Share your progress and journey with others, and if you feel you have more to contribute, pass your skill on to the next generation. Become a mentor or teacher and give thanks every day for the blessing of being able to express yourself, giving your exceptional gift of music to a waiting world!

PLEASE LEAVE A REVIEW

Now that you have everything you need to **excel in playing bass**, it's time to share your newfound knowledge and show other readers where they can find the same guidance.

Simply by leaving your honest opinion of this book on Amazon or wherever you purchased it, you'll help other **bassists** discover the information they're looking for and pass their passion for **playing music** forward.

Thank you for your help. The **passion for playing bass** is kept alive when we pass on our knowledge – and you're helping **me** to do just that.

If you purchased my book on Amazon, here's the link to leave your review:

https://www.amazon.com/review/review-your-purchases/?asin=1966258046

Or, you can just scan this QR code to get to the Amazon review page:

ABOUT THE AUTHOR

Tad Sisler is an American Composer, Author and Producer of feature films and music. More than a thousand of his original works are available through *iTunes, Amazon* and virtually every other major marketplace.

Through the years, **Tad** created and released independent feature films and documentaries, television shows, developed a music store and vast collection of music for film and television usages, in addition to published screenplays and books. **Tad** is a voting member of *The Academy of Recording Arts & Sciences.* **Tad** invented a wireless karaoke all-in-one microphone that became a best-seller on *Amazon.* A child prodigy, Tad was playing advanced piano pieces at the age of 8, and rating superior in Classical piano competitions at 12. Tad won his first scholarship for singing at 12, attending the Idyllwild School of Music and the Arts, then affiliated with the University of Southern California.

FEATURE FILMS

Tad produced, edited, and released "**The Ghosts of Brewer Town**", a mystery feature film, currently available on *YouTube.*

TELEVISION PROJECTS

Tad launched the **Journey To An Extraordinary Life-Legends Among Us** documentary series, which chronicles the lives and careers of legendary artists, actors, sports figures and heroes of medicine, in a feature-film format.

BOOKS

Books, Audio Books and Podcasts released by **Tad** include **"Reflections in the Key of Life-The Steve Madaio Story"**, chronicling the life and times of America's most prolific trumpeter. This book garnered a **Readers' Favorite Book Award** for Tad.

"Mafia Baby" is a shocking true story of a woman raped by a Mafioso, who then raised his child alone. Tad's autobiography, **"It's a Long Climb to The Middle"** *is* available currently on *Amazon* and *Barnes & Noble*. Screenplays in development by Tad Sisler include **"The Incredible Spark of Franklin Benjamin"**, and **"Please Don't Forget"**. **Tad's** latest **Music Mastery** collection of books is designed to educate and inspire musicians to become masters.

MUSIC

Tad's production music catalog tripled in size with the addition of thousands of excellent production music tracks, as well as hundreds of sound-alike tracks for the DJ/Karaoke industry, now distributed on **iTunes, Amazon Marketplace, CD Baby, Spotify, Rdio, Xbox Music** and dozens of other outlets Worldwide.

Tad produced and released "The Barcelona Sessions" to 1000 radio stations Worldwide, with never- before-heard original performances by Miles Davis' bassist, Bill Evan's drummer, Frank Sinatra's saxophonist, Maynard Ferguson's guitarist, and Andrae Crouch' flutist/saxophonist, produced by Tad Sisler in his recording studio.

Tad Sisler composed the full score to **"The Encore Of Tony Duran"**, an indie feature film starring **Elliott Gould, William Katt, Nicki Ziering and Cody Kasch**, along with his co- composer Andrew Fraga, Jr.

After having the distinction of being the first film to sell-out at the prestigious *Palm Springs International Film Festival*, the film won the **Jury Award** for **Best Feature Film** at the *Las Vegas Film Festival* and the *Santa Fe Film Festival*, as well as the **Indie Spirit Award** at the *Fort Lauderdale Film Festival* and the **Audience Favorite Award** at *Tallgrass Film Festival*, in conjunction with a **Lifetime Achievement Award** for **Elliott Gould.** The film is available on *Amazon Prime*.

Tad completed the music and audio editing for the TV Series **"American M.C.".** The first 7 episodes are complete and in the process of distribution through **iTunes**. Tad scored the Main Title theme to **American M.C.** as well as underscore and providing Music Supervision and source music.

PRODUCTION

Tad Sisler has been a valuable member of the team of specialists and project developers for **Yamaha Corporation of America**, delivering hundreds of intricate projects to exact **Yamaha** specifications over a 10 year period.

Tad received accolades in 2011 after being given the honor and challenge of doing the "official" remake of the iconic "**Andy Griffith Theme**" for the estate of the composer **Earle Hagen** as a perfect sound-alike, along with his composing associate Andrew Fraga, Jr.

Following a stint composing for a series entitled "**Famous Families**" on **Foxstar** and working as assistant to composer Jeff Edwards on the television series "**Silk Stalkings**" and "**Renegade**" in the late 1990's, Tad Sisler and founded & developed a production music catalog, containing thousands of high-quality music tracks available for sync licenses in film, television and advertising in more than 150 genres.

In addition to handling Music Supervision on "**The Encore Of Tony Duran**", and on "**American M.C.**", "**The Ghosts of Brewer Town**", "**'Tis' The Season**", the "**Journey To an Extraordinary Life**" series, **Tad** produced the "**It's Everyone Else Who Has A Problem!**" series, and placed his original music on **NBC**, **ABC/Disney**, **Warner Brothers Television**, **TNT**, US National Infomercial campaigns through **Guthy/Renker** and **Script To Screen**, as well as custom composing for the TV and Advertising industry.

Tad released contains hundreds of top-quality soundalike tracks produced by **Tad** and his associates, for DJ and Karaoke usages, currently on *ITunes, Amazon Marketplace, Spotify, Rdio, Xbox Music,* and many other outlets.

LIVE PRODUCTION

In the 1980's and 1990's, **Tad** and his team produced a series of live headliner events at multiple venues from the ground up, including sold-out performances by **Kenny Rogers, Earth, Wind & Fire, Los Lobos, Glen Campbell, The Righteous Brothers, Lou Rawls, Tito Puente,** the **Power Jam** featuring **Timmy T, Tara Kemp, Candyman, Soul To Soul** and more.

HISTORY

As a very young man, Tad Sisler worked as a performer for **Frank Sinatra**. Tad studied music in choreography under world-famous Broadway Dancer/Choreographer **Jacque D'Amboise**, received superior ratings in classical piano performance in tough **Joanna Hodges** international competitions, and received private acting lessons from **Richard Burton**, a friend of his family.

Tad attended the prestigious **Idyllwild School of Music and the Arts** on vocal music scholarships during the period when it was affiliated with the **University of Southern California**.

In High School, Tad was one of 100 statewide vocalists elected to the prestigious **All-State Choir** in Missouri.

During his storied career, Tad has also had the honor of performing with and working among such greats as **Gladys Knight, Rita Coolidge, B.B. King, Marilyn McCoo, Johnny Mathis, Kenny Rogers, Tito Puente, Sonny and Mary Bono, Gene Barry, Teri Cole Whittaker, Shecky Greene, Peter Marshall, Mary Hart, Blackwell, Herb Jeffries, Trini Lopez, Glen Campbell, Jennifer Hudson** and other legends.

Tad Sisler's extensive experience, state of the art facility and history of delivering quality feature films and music <u>on time and on budget</u>, as well as the ability to draw from an extensive catalog of production music, allows his experienced team to offer complete services in custom film and television production as well as in music composition and production efficiently.

Tad is proud and humbled to be a voting member of the **Academy of Recording Arts & Sciences**, which allows him to have a voice to vote for great artists worthy of winning a **Grammy Award**. Many of Tad's works have been placed into Grammy consideration.

In 2023, Tad won a prestigious **Telly Award** for creative excellence in his *Journey to an Extraordinary Life* film series.

Modern Renaissance Publishing is at the forefront of a new intellectual awakening, dedicated to fostering a renaissance of ideas that resonate in today's world. Our mission is to bring cutting-edge concepts and timeless wisdom to the public through a diverse array of publishing formats, including books, eBooks, and audiobooks.

We are proud to launch our **Music Mastery** series, offering comprehensive guides and insights for musicians of all levels. In addition to our literary endeavors, we also publish original music, enriching the cultural landscape with creative expressions.

Whether you're seeking to expand your knowledge, enhance your skills, or simply be inspired, **Modern Renaissance Publishing** provides the resources and content to empower your journey. Join us as we bridge the rich heritage of the past with the innovative spirit of the present to shape a brighter, more enlightened future.

REFERENCES

License link to all Wikimedia Commons and Creative Commons photo credit references: Creative Commons. (n.d.). *Attribution-ShareAlike 4.0 International (CC BY-SA 4.0)* [License]. Retrieved from https://creativecommons.org/licenses/by-sa/4.0/

AllMusic. (n.d.). *Carol Kaye*. AllMusic. Retrieved from https://www.allmusic.com/artist/carol-kaye-mn0000174041

AzQuotes. (n.d.). *Charles Mingus Quotes*. Retrieved from https://www.azquotes.com/author/10172-Charles_Mingus

AzQuotes. (n.d.). *Rod Stewart Quotes*. Retrieved from https://www.azquotes.com/author/14138-Rod_Stewart

AzQuotes. (n.d.). *John Patitucci Quotes*. Retrieved from https://www.azquotes.com/author/85549-John_Patitucci

AzQuotes. (n.d.). *Carol Kaye Quotes*. Retrieved from https://www.azquotes.com/author/63651-Carol_Kaye

AzQuotes. (n.d.). *Nathan East Quotes*. Retrieved from https://www.azquotes.com/author/40832-Nathan_East

AzQuotes. (n.d.). *Metronome Quotes*. Retrieved from https://www.azquotes.com/quotes/topics/metronomes.html

BrainyQuote. (n.d.). *Flea Quotes*. Retrieved from https://www.brainyquote.com/authors/flea-quotes#:~:text=Music%20is%20like%20the%20genius,of%20it%20in%20their%20lives.&text=I%20wanted%20to%20play%20in,I%20dedicated%20my%20life%20to.

BrainyQuote. (n.d.). *Kenny Rogers Quotes*. Retrieved from https://www.brainyquote.com/search_results?q=Kenny+rogers

BrainyQuote. (n.d.). *Glen Campbell Quotes*. Retrieved from https://www.brainyquote.com/search_results?x=0&y=0&q=glen+campbell

BrainyQuote. (n.d.). *Jaco Pastorius Quotes*. Retrieved from https://www.brainyquote.com/search_results?x=0&y=0&q=jaco+pastorius

BrainyQuote. (n.d.). *Stanley Clarke Quotes*. Retrieved from https://www.brainyquote.com/search_results?x=0&y=0&q=Stanley+Clarke

BrainyQuote. (n.d.). *Jack Kemp Quotes*. Retrieved from https://www.brainyquote.com/search_results?x=0&y=0&q=jack+kemp

BrainyQuote. (n.d.). *Roger Waters Quotes*. Retrieved from https://www.brainyquote.com/search_results?x=0&y=0&q=ROGER+WATERS

BrainyQuote. (n.d.). *Geddy Lee Quotes*. Retrieved from https://www.brainyquote.com/search_results?x=0&y=0&q=geddy+lee

BrainyQuote. (n.d.). *Tony Levin Quotes.* Retrieved from
https://www.brainyquote.com/search_results?x=0&y=0&q=TONY+LEVI
N

BrainyQuote. (n.d.). *Bill Medley Quotes.* Retrieved from
https://www.brainyquote.com/search_results?x=0&y=0&q=bill+medley

BrainyQuote. (n.d.). *Magic Johnson Quotes.* Retrieved from
https://www.brainyquote.com/search_results?x=0&y=0&q=magic+johnson

BrainyQuote. (n.d.). *Les Claypool Quotes.* Retrieved from
https://www.brainyquote.com/search_results?x=0&y=0&q=LES+CLAYP
OOL

BrainyQuote. (n.d.). *Trini Lopez Quotes.* Retrieved from
https://www.brainyquote.com/authors/trini-lopez-quotes

BrainyQuote. (n.d.). *Donald "Duck" Dunn Quotes.* Retrieved from
https://www.brainyquote.com/authors/donald-dunn-quotes

BrainyQuote. (n.d.). *Bass Player Quotes.* Retrieved from
https://www.brainyquote.com/topics/bassist-quotes

BrainyQuote. (n.d.). *Sting Quotes.* Retrieved from
https://www.brainyquote.com/search_results?x=0&y=0&q=STING

BrainyQuote. (n.d.). *Cliff Burton Quotes.* Retrieved from
https://www.brainyquote.com/search_results?x=0&y=0&q=CLIFF+BURT
ON

BrainyQuote. (n.d.). *Geezer Butler Quotes.* Retrieved from
https://www.brainyquote.com/search_results?x=0&y=0&q=GEEZER+BU
TLER

BrainyQuote. (n.d.). *Jack Bruce Quotes.* Retrieved from
https://www.brainyquote.com/search_results?x=0&y=0&q=jack+bruce

BrainyQuote. (n.d.). *Chris Squire Quotes.* Retrieved from
https://www.brainyquote.com/search_results?x=0&y=0&q=chris+squire

BrainyQuote. (n.d.). *Snoop Dogg Quotes.* Retrieved from
https://www.brainyquote.com/search_results?x=23&y=6&q=snoop+dogg

BrainyQuote. (n.d.). *George H. W. Bush Quotes.* Goodreads. Retrieved
from
https://www.goodreads.com/author/quotes/579816.George_H_W_Bush

Essay Wizards. (n.d.). *Sergio Mendes Quotes.* Retrieved from
https://www.essaywizards.com/quotes/authors/sergio_mendes/

Gollihur Music. (n.d.). *Upright Bass Buyer's Guide (Especially for First-
Time Buyers).* Retrieved from https://gollihurmusic.com/upright-bass-
buyers-guide-especially-for-first-time-buyers/

Impactidy Arts. (2012, July 9). *Marshall Hawkins Profile: Impact May
2012.* Retrieved from

https://impactidyarts.wordpress.com/2012/07/09/marshall-hawkins-profile-impact-may-2012/

Kyere-Boateng, R., & Marek, M. (2021). Analysis of the social-ecological causes of deforestation and forest degradation in Ghana: Application of the DPSIR framework. *Forests, 12*(4), 409.

LinkedIn. (n.d.). McCallum, M. *The Most Dangerous Quote: "You Do What You Love for a Living."* Retrieved from https://www.linkedin.com/pulse/most-dangerous-quote-you-do-what-love-living-marlene-mccallum/

MusicRadar. (n.d.). *How to Become a Session Bassist: Top Tips from Leland Sklar, Sandy Beales, and More.* Retrieved from https://www.musicradar.com/news/how-to-become-a-session-bassist-top-tips-from-leland-sklar-sandy-beales-and-more

NPR. (2000, June 15). *Carol Kaye: Studio Great.* Retrieved from https://www.npr.org/2000/06/15/1075473/carol-kaye-studio-great

Reddit. (2020). *Here is a James Jamerson Quote I Found Very Inspiring.* Retrieved from https://www.reddit.com/r/Bass/comments/epvob1/here_is_a_james_jamersons_quote_i_found_very/

Frontiers in Psychology. (n.d.). Retrieved from https://www.frontiersin.org/journals/psychology

Neurodegeneration Research. (2017, September). *Uncovering Why Playing a Musical Instrument Can Protect Brain Health.* Retrieved from https://neurodegenerationresearch.eu/2017/09/uncovering-why-playing-a-musical-instrument-can-protect-brain-health/

UPI. (2024, January 28). *Playing Instrument Can Boost Brain Health.* Retrieved from https://www.upi.com/Health_News/2024/01/28/playing-instrument-brain-health/9851706260072/

John Bonham. (n.d.). *John Paul Jones Quotes.* Retrieved from https://johnbonham.co.uk/quotes/johnpauljones-quotes.html

QuoteFancy. (n.d.). *Leland Sklar Quotes.* Retrieved from https://quotefancy.com/leland-sklar-quotes

ERIC. (n.d.). *EJ1356962.* Retrieved from https://eric.ed.gov/?id=EJ1356962

Making Music Mag. (n.d.). *Tips from the Pros: How to Prepare for a Live Performance.* Retrieved from https://makingmusicmag.com/tips-from-the-pros-how-to-prepare-for-a-live-performance/

Victor Wooten. (n.d.). *Victor Wooten Official Site.* Retrieved from https://www.victorwooten.com/

Neaera. (n.d.). *Guitar.* Retrieved from https://neaera.com/guitar/

AzQuotes. (n.d.). *Kim Deal Quotes.* Retrieved from
https://www.azquotes.com/author/41935-Kim_Deal
BrainyQuote. (n.d.). *Mary Tyler Moore Quotes.* Retrieved from
https://www.brainyquote.com/search_results?x=0&y=0&q=mary+tyler+m
oore
BrainyQuote. (n.d.). *Colin Powell Quotes.* Retrieved from
https://www.brainyquote.com/search_results?x=0&y=0&q=colin+powell
YouTube. (2023). *[Journey To an Extraordinary Life-Tad Sisler and
Louie Stevens].* YouTube. https://www.youtube.com/watch?v=-
wYCSRDyIic
ScienceDaily. (2024, January 29). *Playing an instrument boosts brain's
executive function, study finds.* ScienceDaily.
https://www.sciencedaily.com/releases/2024/01/240129122415.htm
AZ Quotes. (n.d.). *Elliott Gould quotes.* AZ Quotes.
https://www.azquotes.com/author/31289-Elliott_Gould

MODERN RENAISSANCE
PUBLISHING

www.ingramcontent.com/pod-product-compliance
Lightning Source LLC
Chambersburg PA
CBHW060937120626
46557CB00003B/1039